THE BATTLE
OF AACHEN

Irving Werstein

THE BATTLE
OF AACHEN

MAPS BY AVA MORGAN

Thomas Y. Crowell Company : New York

This book is dedicated
to the United States Infantry
and especially to the 5th Infantry Regiment
in which I served from January 6, 1942,
until March 10, 1945

AUTHOR'S NOTE

This book deals with an important, but little noticed, phase of the operations in the European Theater during World War II—the American First Army's capture of Aachen, Germany, and the breaching of the Siegfried line. The Battle of Aachen lasted more than a month (September 13, 1944—October 21, 1944). It consisted of many fierce clashes in the Aachen area between defending Germans and attacking Americans. Some of the war's deadliest fighting took place during those few weeks.

Aachen was the first major German city to be attacked by American ground forces. The German Fuehrer, Adolph Hitler, swore to hold Aachen and promised his people that not "one inch of sacred German soil" would fall to the Americans. Since the city was a key bastion of the Siegfried line—a network of fortified positions Hitler had built to defend the western borders of Germany—U. S. troops had to break the Siegfried line in order to capture the city.

The Battle of Aachen was divided into two main American efforts. The first was to encircle the city and isolate it from the rest of Germany. The second, to beat back German reinforcements trying to lift the siege.

The story of Aachen, which I have here sought to re-create, is a saga of indomitable American determination. Seldom have Americans been called upon to endure such hardships and dangers as they faced in the struggle for Aachen. I have tried to depict the Germans fairly and objectively. The German soldiers were tenacious and brave—but theirs was an evil cause. The Germany Hitler had created was destroyed, as it should have been, by free men of every race, creed, and color. The last act in the German tragedy started at Aachen.

I have simplified the telling of the battle; it would have been impossible to include every detail in such a book. If I have glossed over the role played by individual units, I apologize. Every American GI who fought at Aachen deserves credit; and I now wish to acknowledge the part each played in gaining the objective.

It is my hope that I have done more than merely re-count military history. My purpose was to depict the horror and futility of war without disparaging the brave young men on both sides who fought and died at Aachen.

In gathering the material for this work, I interviewed men who served at Aachen with the U. S. First Army. I also consulted diaries, journals, letters, and memoirs, both German and American. Official records of the U. S. First Army and the 1st Division were made available to me. As always in a project of this sort, I found that among my most valuable sources were the contemporary news-papers and magazines—especially those two wonderful Army publications, *Yank, The Army Weekly Magazine;* and the Army daily, *Stars and Stripes.* Published histories of various divisions and regiments which participated in the Aachen campaign were also helpful.

Of course, many people assisted me in gathering data for this book. I owe thanks to Mr. Sherrod East and Mr. Philip Bower, Chief Archivist and Acting Chief Archivist, National Archives and Records Service, World War II Records Division, Alexandria, Virginia, for providing records of the 1st Division. Mr. Arthur L. Chaitt, of Philadelphia, Corresponding Secretary of the Society of the 1st Division, generously sent me a copy of *Danger Forward,* the division history.

Mr. George Mandel (ex-Sergeant, 113th Armored Cavalry Reconnaissance Battalion), a New Yorker who fought at Aachen, and Mr. Joseph Ferguson (ex-Sergeant, 175th Infantry, 29th Division) helped immeasurably with personal narratives.

Mr. John Augustin, United States Information Agency, Washington, D. C., regaled me with stirring accounts of the action around Aachen. I can never amply thank Mr. Charles E. Dornbusch, Military Historian of the New York Public Library, who assiduously and faithfully led me to the right source material; nor can I sufficiently show my gratitude to Mr. Bruce Jacobs, New York City, without whom I would have followed many false trails.

The staff of the American History Room, New York

AUTHOR'S NOTE

Public Library, was unfailingly cooperative as were Dr. James J. Heslin and the librarians at the New-York Historical Society.

I must also express appreciation to my wife for her patience and to my seven-year-old son for steering clear of his favorite playmate during working hours.

I. W.

CONTENTS

"German soldiers! Heroes of Aachen! Our Fuehrer calls upon you to defend to the last bullet, the last gasp of breath, Aachen, this jewel city of German kultur, this shrine where German emperors and kings have been enthroned! Germans! Soldiers of the Third Reich! Drive out the American gangsters! Drown them in their own blood! The Fuehrer and the German people are counting on you! Heil Hitler! Sieg Heil!"

Heinrich Himmler, September, 1944, to the German garrison defending Aachen.

"People of Aachen! Force your leaders to stop this useless bloodshed and destruction! German soldiers! You are surrounded, outnumbered, cut off from food and ammunition! Your situation is hopeless! Further resistance is useless! Surrender now! Tomorrow may be too late! You have only one choice—immediate honorable surrender or annihilation!"

Ultimatum to Aachen, October 10, 1944, by Lieutenant General Courtney H. Hodges, commanding the U. S. First Army.

I. THE SITUATION

GERMANY,
1944

HITLER'S WORLD
SUMMER, 1942

CHAPTER I

On a fateful morning in September, 1939, Hitler's armies lunged across the borders of Poland to start the Second World War. Since that day Germany had overrun a dozen nations. The Nazi swastika waved from the Arctic Circle to the shores of Greece. German soldiers strutted from the English Channel to the Black Sea.

In Germany itself, eight million foreign captives labored as slaves in factories and fields. For other millions, the Nazis had set up "death camps" where unspeakable horrors were inflicted on helpless victims. In all history such organized barbarism had never before been known.

"Today we conquer Germany! Tomorrow the world!" This was Hitler's promise to his followers.

No man had ever come closer to realizing his ambitions. For a time, Hitler seemed to have succeeded; but only for a time. He had started the war in a burst of glorious victories. Now the specter of defeat haunted Hitler's Germany.

In June, 1941, the Fuehrer had turned on Soviet Russia. His troops had marched triumphantly into the U.S.S.R. only to meet disaster at Stalingrad during the winter of 1942–43. Now, in 1944, the Russians were advancing from the east, and German armies had to fall back before the Soviet onslaught. The Nazis were fighting for their lives on the Eastern Front. And as if this struggle was not enough, Hitler was faced with disaster from the west.

On June 6, 1944, an armada of warships protected by hundreds of aircraft had successfully carried British and American troops across the English Channel to landings on the Normandy beaches of France. Hitler had bragged that the fortifications he had built on the French coast were impregnable. But the Allied attack on D-Day could not be stopped. Nothing could save the Germans in Normandy.

The Germans were caught in the giant vise of a two-front war. The English and Americans were pressing from the west and the Russians were clamping down from the east. The huge Allied pincers were crushing the life out of Germany.

But the Nazi war machine was still strong. Germany

launched V-1 and V-2 rocket bombs from sites in northern Belgium and Holland to rain death and havoc on London. The Luftwaffe (German Air Force) had jet fighter planes better than any Allied aircraft. The Wehrmacht (German Army) still had fighting strength.

That summer the Nazis faced yet another threat in the lands they had conquered. Despite Hitler's Gestapo (Secret Police), neither torture, execution squads, nor death camps could snuff out freedom's flame. Wherever the Nazis had invaded, brave men and women had risked their lives to strike back. Partisans rose behind the German lines. Here they ambushed a patrol. There a sentry was knifed, an ammunition train blown up, a bridge destroyed. The Germans bled from ten thousand tiny wounds that weakened them for the Allied counterthrusts.

In Africa, the German Desert Fox, General Erwin Rommel, and his Afrika Korps had been smashed by the British and Americans. This led to the Allied invasion of Italy. In September, 1943, Italy surrendered, and Hitler no longer had a major ally to help him.

Germany itself shuddered under the impact of constant aerial bombings by the British Royal Air Force and the U. S. Army Air Corps. At night, RAF bombers ranged across the Fatherland, and scores of great German cities were ravaged to avenge Rotterdam, London, Coventry, and Warsaw. During daylight hours, American planes winged deep into the Reich and dropped their one-thousand-pound blockbusters.

The German U-boats (submarines), which once had menaced Atlantic shipping lanes by hunting in wolf packs and sinking merchant vessels, were themselves being stalked by fighting ships equipped with modern sub-destroying devices. Allied convoys now plied the ocean without fear of the undersea menace.

The dread German war machine that had terrorized the free world and dominated Europe, the whole Nazi apparatus of death camps, Gestapo, SS (Elite Corps), which had promised doom to all mankind, now faced destruction at the hands of the intended victims.

At the end of summer, 1944, in the fifth year of World War II, the vise was closing around Germany, the nation Adolph Hitler had sworn would last "a thousand years."

2. PRELUDE TO ATTACK

BILDCHEN, GERMANY
Sunday, September 10, 1944

EUROPE

SUMMER, 1939

CHAPTER 2

AT 6:00 A.M., Sunday, September 10, 1944, as it had for decades, the clock in the church steeple of Bildchen, a tiny German frontier village, began tolling the hour. Villagers still abed stirred sleepily when the chimes echoed in the warm morning stillness. The sound they made was a comforting one to the Bildcheners. Their village lay 1,500 yards from the Belgian border, and the clock bell reassured them that some things never changed even in war-torn Europe where life had been turned topsy-turvy.

As the bell tolled its fifth reverberating stroke, an explosion shattered the calm. The church steeple collapsed in a shower of mortar dust and bricks. The clock had been silenced forever.

9

Startled people, still in their night clothes, fled into the street. Suddenly the air was filled with fierce *whooshing* noises. A series of explosions rocked the village. Several houses began to burn.

"Artillery!" someone screamed.

"The Americans are shelling us!"

The Bildcheners fled in panic to nearby woods and fields, hugging the ground as more and still more shells pounded their village into rubble.

After five years of war, the villagers had grown used to air raids, especially in recent months, since RAF and U. S. Army planes now often bombed Aachen, a large, fortified city only a few kilometers northeast of Bildchen.

This was different. The enemy's planes could drop bombs while his troops were still far away, but even the dullest person knew an artillery bombardment meant the Americans were close at hand with their tanks, cannon, and soldiers.

It must have mattered little to the Bildcheners that a historical event was taking place in their obscure hamlet that morning. This was the first time in more than a century that enemy cannon had pounded German soil. Only an accident of geography had gained that dubious distinction for Bildchen. The village happened to be located in the path of the U. S. First Army, which was coming to capture Aachen.

The shelling was being carried out by a battery of U. S. 155-mm (Long Tom) howitzers posted in an orchard on a hillside near a Belgian village ten miles away. The big guns were firing at their extreme range. American gunners peering into range finders knew this was no ordinary firing mission, for, as the morning mists cleared, an officer scanning the rolling terrain through his binoculars had announced, "Boys, that's Germany up yonder! Let's shake it up a little!"

"Won't the Krauts be surprised when we hit 'em. I bet Hitler never told them they'd have days like this!" An artillery spotter chuckled.

The section's Number One cannon was loaded with a shell upon which someone had chalked, "To Hell with Hitler!" A gunner stood ready to yank the lanyard when so ordered.

"Number One! Maximum elevation! Deflection right one-zero! One round HE (high explosive)! Fire!" the battery commander cried.

The gunner pulled the lanyard. A jarring noise shook the ground. Flame lanced through the muzzle smoke. The TNT-filled shell sped on its destructive flight to Bildchen.

"Battery fire at will!" the commander shouted.

The men paused only long enough to cheer as pillars of smoke rose from the distant target. Then they went to work in earnest. The bombardment of Bildchen continued until the battery was ordered to move on. The Long Toms, their huge caterpillar treads raising clouds of powdery dust, clanked on toward the German border.

The shells fired from that Belgian hillside did more than pound Bildchen into dust. They were the opening shots of what proved to be one of the most fiercely fought en-

11

gagements of World War II—the Battle of Aachen, the first important city inside Germany to be attacked by American troops.

The battle that was shaping up had resulted from a series of disastrous German defeats in France and Belgium during July and August. The Nazis were driven from those two countries which they had occupied since 1940 by a smashing U. S. offensive led by the VII Corps of the First Army under General Courtney Hodges.

Thousands of Germans had been killed, wounded, or captured during the American drive. Now the beaten enemy was fleeing behind his own borders. When Hodges pressed on, the Germans decided to make a stand at Aachen as ordered to do by Hitler.

"The Americans must not be permitted to cross Germany's border! We shall destroy them at Aachen!" Hitler had ranted.

If the German frontier could be defended, Aachen was the best place to make a fight. This the Americans were soon to discover.

3. THE BATTLEGROUND

AACHEN, GERMANY
September, 1944

"THE RED BALL LINE"

CHAPTER 3

Aachen—which the French called Aix-la-Chapelle and the Dutch, Aken—had been regarded by Germans with reverence for centuries. The ancient city, founded in the eighth century A.D., was believed to be both birthplace and burial ground of Charlemagne, greatest of the early German emperors. During his reign he made Aachen the seat of Western culture and learning. At Aachen, Charlemagne built a palace which later became the site of a magnificent cathedral where, through the ages, thirty-two German kings and emperors had been crowned.

In modern times, Aachen had developed industrially rather than culturally. By 1944, it was a city of 165,000.

Along the Dutch frontier northwest of Aachen were rich coal fields; all around the city were busy factories producing cloth, glass, pins, and needles.

In addition to this business activity, Aachen was popular as a health resort and spa to which tourists flocked for the hot sulphur baths and medicinal mineral waters. Aachen had many hotels, shops, public gardens, squares, and parks. Elegant apartments lined its fashionable streets.

The war had not touched Aachen until 1943, when Allied bombers began to attack it; but the raids had not been too bad. The bombers aimed at the industrial districts on the city's outskirts. Aachen itself suffered little serious damage. For five years the fighting had been far away, and the smug Aacheners never believed that one day the enemy would be on the doorstep.

From a military angle, Aachen made an excellent defensive position. North and west of the city ran a series of fortified razorbacked ridges which dominated the terrain. To the southeast the approaches to Aachen were guarded by more ridges and hills. But the ridges were the least redoubtable of its defenses. The city was a virtual fortress, a key bastion of the Westwall, a defensive system built by Hitler to guard Germany's western frontier in 1939–40.

Better known as the Siegfried line, named after the mythical German hero, the Westwall was a continuous series of machine-gun emplacements, pillboxes, concrete blockhouses, antitank ditches, barbed wire, and mine fields that ran all the way from the Dutch frontier to the

Swiss border. The Siegfried line guarded Germany from any invasion mounted by the Western Allies.

At Aachen, the line was further strengthened by stone walls, booby traps, and rows of deep ditches. German thoroughness and efficiency had gone into every foot of the Westwall. Where natural barriers existed, such as the river north of Aachen, gun emplacements cleverly hugged the river lines.

The concrete installations were strongly built. The pill-boxes stood twenty to thirty feet high and were twenty to twenty-five feet wide by forty to fifty feet deep. At least half of every emplacement was underground with living quarters for six to eight men. These concrete "forts" were armed with 37-mm antitank cannon, both light and heavy machine guns, and the rapid-firing weapons of the men in the bunkers.

Staggered rows of pointed concrete obstacles, called dragon teeth, were liberally sprinkled before each position. They had been implanted to impede tanks and other armored vehicles, slowing them down so they were made vulnerable to antitank weapons. In the Aachen region, every border town and village was part of the Siegfried line. What appeared to be thatched-roof peasant cottages or pleasant farmhouses were really artfully camouflaged machine-gun nests with walls of reinforced concrete five to eight feet thick. In some sectors, the line had been laid out to a depth of fifteen to twenty-five kilometers. Breaking the Siegfried line was a formidable assignment for any invader.

Since Aachen guarded a broad plain that led to Cologne

and the Rhine River forty miles to the east, the Westwall's designers built the fortifications strongest in that area, the gateway to the Rhineland.

Apparently the Germans had considered every detail when building the Siegfried line. Under normal circumstances no enemy could hope to penetrate into Germany through the Westwall without suffering such fantastic losses that he would be vulnerable to a counterattack. However, the situation for the Germans was far from normal in September, 1944.

Not even the most astute German general could have foretold the debacle which had befallen the Wehrmacht in France and Belgium during July, August, and early September. As a result of the hectic German retreat, the commander of the U. S. First Army, General Courtney Hodges, believed he could reach Aachen and sweep through the Siegfried line before the disorganized enemy was able to man his defenses.

The American general gambled on the speed with which his highly mobile army could move. He issued an order that boiled down to the single idea: "Beat the Germans to Aachen. Keep going until you reach the Rhine River!"

The pace-setter in this grueling race was the VII Corps, First Army, which hurtled full tilt down the Liége-Herve-Battice-Aachen road. Tanks of its 3rd Armored Division sped along, the exhausted crewmen napping in the jolting vehicles and eating cold C rations. The infantrymen of the 1st Infantry Division were crammed into trucks which careened down the highway in roaring convoys at breakneck speed to Aachen on the German frontier.

A war correspondent traveling with the division wrote:

"The men believe the enemy is on the ropes and that a solid haymaker will put the Nazis down for the count. These GIs need no urging to push ahead. They feel the end of the war is in sight—and every man forces himself to the limit. Victory is a prize worth winning. . . ."

The 1st Division's code name was DANGER—a word which appropriately described an outfit that through two World Wars had lived up to the motto: "No mission too difficult! No sacrifice too great! Duty first!" Men who wore the 1st Division shoulder patch (a large red figure one) in 1944 advanced through regions of northern France and Belgium where the 1st Division had fought the Germans in 1918.

Danger had been the 1st Division's constant companion since November, 1942, when the previously unblooded unit landed in North Africa. Now the men faced worse dangers than any they had experienced before.

The Siegfried line loomed before them—but even the greenest replacements who had yet to fight a battle raced ahead without doubts or qualms. Both rookies and veterans believed nothing could stop the Big Red One, as they fondly called their division. The men who had been in combat had defeated Hitler's best troops. Even the SS had run from them. During the advance across France and Belgium they had corralled thousands of Nazis into the POW pens.

Such men were not impressed by what they had heard of the Siegfried line. They feared neither pillboxes, machine-gun nests, booby traps, mine fields, nor dragon teeth.

A GI laughed. "Hell, all we have to do is send a couple of dentists to yank out the dragon teeth and we'll tie knots in the Siegfried line."

Everything seemed to favor the Americans. The weather was bright and sunny, cool enough for comfort, perfect flying weather for the Army Air Corps to hammer the Germans daily on the ground and in the air. The U. S. Army Air Corps ruled the skies, the Luftwaffe was taking a terrible whipping. In one day, American flyers destroyed 105 German planes—79 in the air, the rest on the ground.

Just as U. S. planes dominated the air, U. S. infantry, artillery, and armor ruled the land. Small wonder that every GI in the 1st Division—in every division—of the First Army was certain of victory. The Americans pushed on to the German frontier with songs, laughter, and jokes, as though bound for a picnic rather than a battle.

Morale was high when the VII Corps deployed to assault the Siegfried line at Aachen. The 1st Infantry Division held the left flank, the 9th Infantry Division the right, while the 3rd Armored Division supported both. The rest of the First Army wheeled into position on the German frontier: the XIX Corps north of the VII Corps, the V Corps south of it.

From Aachen in the north to Nancy in the south, Hitler's Westwall was under siege; the fury of free men was about to fall on Germany. In the conquered nations of Europe, in America, in the whole free world, men and women prayed that the long, terrible war might soon be ended.

Their prayers were not without basis: In the Pacific the Americans were taking island after island, moving ever closer to Japan itself; in Europe the Germans seemed to be staggering. Perhaps the world might not have to face another agonizing winter of war. Perhaps, even before 1944 ended, the Germans would be beaten and, as in the then-current popular song, the lights would "go on again all over the world."

This vision of victory in the West dimmed just as the Americans prepared to attack the Westwall and invade Germany. A grave defect in the U. S. armies was exposed by the swift and spectacular advance to the German border.

Because the American advance had been so rapid, the Services of Supply (SOS) could not keep up with the rapidly thrusting armies. The First Army, especially, had raced ahead so speedily that supplies were two or three days behind the forward elements. Supply lines that reached back four hundred miles to Normandy were stretched to the breaking point.

U. S. armor and infantry had to stop at the Siegfried line because forward units were out of fuel, food, ammunition, and medical supplies.

Tank commanders frantically radioed headquarters: "Gas low! Send more or we can't keep rolling!" But headquarters had no gasoline, and without it, tank motors spluttered and died. Vehicles carrying the GIs who were racing the Germans for Aachen also ran out of gasoline and the pursuit had to be continued on foot.

This development allowed many Germans who might otherwise have been cut off and captured to reach the pillboxes and machine-gun nests of the Siegfried line. If a lack of supplies had not stalled the Americans, they probably could have swarmed through the Westwall to the banks of the Rhine River, forty miles to the east, without difficulty. Aachen would have fallen at the first American thrust. As late as September 10, when U. S. howitzers shelled Bildchen, the Siegfried line was poorly manned. Pillboxes that were meant to hold eight men had only two or three available to defend them. Unfortunately, the U. S. First Army could push no farther. Its vehicles were immobilized. The big artillery guns had no shells to shoot. Frustrated infantrymen watched in helpless rage as the enemy slipped away from them.

This was happening all along the western front wherever U. S. troops had debouched on Germany's border, as American offensive power waned. The situation was so critical that artillery batteries were obliged to ration shells. Some units could allow only three rounds per gun per day to be fired. Every American weapon from pistols to Long Tom howitzers lacked ammunition. Cartridges had to be doled out to front-line riflemen. If the Germans had not been so disorganized and had been able to counterattack, the Americans would have suffered a disaster. Fortunately for General Hodges, the enemy was not.

The U. S. shortages at the front were not due to any

lack of matériel in the rear. The simple truth was that the American Army had outstripped its ability to supply the troops. The SOS could not contend with the surge of the combat units.

However, the men responsible for supplying the front met the challenge. "We couldn't leave those boys sitting on Germany's threshold without the stuff they needed to blast the Krauts," a supply officer recalled. "So we slashed red tape and chucked the book out the window. We couldn't handle this situation according to regulations."

Every available truck was brought to rear supply depots and loaded with gasoline, shells, cartridges, medical goods, and rations. Convoys of huge six-by-six trailers sped to the front four hundred miles away. Day and night the trucks rolled. "It was like a bucket brigade on wheels," a motor-pool dispatcher said. "Loaded trucks highballed eastward and empties came roaring back for more stuff."

"The Red Ball Line," the GIs dubbed the mobile supply system, because in railroad slang a "red ball" describes an express train that makes no stops until its destination is reached. French, Belgian, and Luxembourg roads were jammed with trucks racing at top speed through towns and villages. Pop-eyed natives gawked at the endless lines of vehicles.

"Les Américains," a gray-bearded French peasant muttered and tapped his forehead with a finger. "They are mad."

At night, despite blackout regulations, truck headlights stabbed through the darkness. Nobody seemed to mind that the beams might bring on German air raids.

"You have to see the road, and you can't deliver the goods if you're wrapped around a tree. We figure if a Kraut plane spots us, there's a fifty-fifty chance he'll miss. But if you run a six-by into a ditch, you're a goner, especially if you happen to be carrying high explosives. So we drive with our lights on," a truck driver told a *New York Times* war correspondent at the time.

The Red Ball Line ran twenty-four hours a day. Drivers barely snatched a few hours to eat and sleep before starting another trip. Despite the pace, there were few accidents, and most of the matériel got through. The truckers knew the American effort hinged on them. In a few days, enough supplies had been hauled up to permit the First Army to open the assault on Aachen and the Siegfried line, although some shortages remained critical, especially in heavy-caliber artillery shells.

"We had plenty of bad days," a supply officer remembered. "Days when I studied my supply charts and wondered if we'd have to throw rocks instead of shells at the Krauts."

4. THE ATTACK

ROTGEN, GERMANY
Wednesday, September 13, 1944

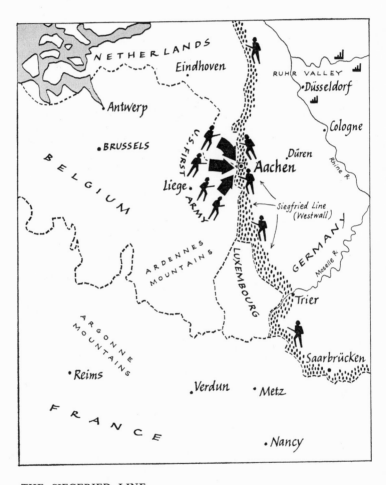

THE SIEGFRIED LINE

CHAPTER 4

O<small>N MONDAY, SEPTEMBER</small> 11, advance elements of the U. S. 1st Division sent patrols across the German border at Bildchen and several other points. But because of the lack of supplies no attempt was made to open a full-scale attack. Every major American unit in the Aachen area had to hold back, instead of pressing the foe.

This breathing spell gave the Germans the chance to recover from the terrible mauling they had been taking since July 26. Reinforcements poured into Aachen from the interior of Germany. The citadel's defenders were exhorted to stand fast in the face of the coming onslaught. Nazi leaders harangued the troops.

"When the foe reaches our positions he must be met by fanatical resistance! Not one inch of our sacred soil must be given up without a struggle! Heil Hitler!" the Nazi party head in the Aachen-Cologne region declared.

The Commander-in-Chief of the German Armies, Field Marshal Gerd von Rundstedt, broadcast to the soldiers at Aachen: "Brave comrades of the Western Front! I expect you to defend Germany to the very last breath of life!"

Hitler's favorite, Field Marshal Walther Model, made a personal visit to inspect the Aachen garrison and said:

"None of us gives up a square foot of German soil while still alive! Whoever . . . retreats without giving battle . . . is a traitor to his people. Soldiers! Our homeland, the lives of our women and children are at stake! The Fuehrer and our loved ones have faith in their soldiers! Long live Germany! Long live the Fuehrer!"

Everyone knew this fiery oratory was propaganda to stiffen the Germans in the Siegfried line. But no one knew better than the Nazi leaders that words were not enough. Besides ringing appeals, Heinrich Himmler, the icy Gestapo chief and Hitler's faithful executioner, gave warning:

"We will not tolerate deserters! Every deserter will find his just punishment. You may count on that! Also, his craven behavior will bring our retribution on his entire family. All blood kin of deserters from our ranks will be rounded up and shot without trial. . . ."

Thus, with speeches and threats, the Germans braced to meet the Americans. Although not every position in the Siegfried line could be properly manned, the German defenses, particularly around Aachen, were very strong. Every available soldier had been rushed into the pillboxes to face the Americans. Cooks, clerks, bakers, and invalided troops were thrown into the breaches. But even these second- and third-rate troops were dangerous. A man did not have to be particularly well trained or in the best physical condition to fire a machine gun from inside a concrete emplacement with eight-foot-thick walls at an unprotected foe.

By drawing troops from other fronts, the German High Command managed to mobilize impressive forces for the defense of Aachen. Hitler had personally supervised the High Command's efforts. He warned that Aachen had to be held at any cost.

In a sweeping order and with disastrous results, Hitler conscripted boys fifteen to eighteen years old and men from fifty to sixty years of age into what was known as the Volkssturm (People's Guards). These hastily trained units were rushed to the front.

"Cannon fodder!" veteran troops called them.

Universities, high schools, factories, and offices were drained to fill the Volkssturm ranks. Hitler had reached the bottom of his manpower pool. Albert Speer, the Nazi Minister of Labor, argued against this step. He pointed out to Hitler that the loss of so many workers would cripple German arms production. Hitler disregarded Speer's logic. "Germany must be defended. I will safeguard the Fatherland with anyone who has the strength to pull a trigger!" the Fuehrer said. "I will defend Germany to the last! No German shall be allowed to stand aside in this death struggle. Any man, woman, or child who will not sacrifice for the Fatherland is a traitor and shall pay a traitor's price!"

"But, my Fuehrer, some of our most skilled people have been taken by the Volkssturm. Is not a tool and die maker more valuable at his bench than with a rifle in his hands?"

"Silence! I will decide who is needed and where he is needed. I am the Fuehrer! I control the destiny of Germany and of all Germans! You will never again question any decision of mine. Understood?" Hitler cried, glaring at Speer.

"Very well, my Fuehrer," Speer meekly said.

Later, Speer wrote in his diary: ". . . this mad conscription crippled our war production. . . . Never again were we to produce at maximum. . . . In some plants production nearly came to a standstill. . . . What Allied bombers had failed to accomplish, Hitler did with a stroke of his pen. . . ."

In obedience to Hitler's ukase that Aachen must be defended "to the last man and the last cartridge," Colonel Gerhardt Wilck, who commanded the city's garrison, ordered every civilian put to work digging trenches and antitank ditches. Grandmothers and old men toiled long hours with pick and shovel as schoolchildren labored alongside them.

The German General Staff believed that the U. S. First Army had the capture of Aachen as its immediate objective. Working on this assumption, Field Marshal Walther Model concentrated his troops to the south and the southeast, the direction from which he anticipated the Americans would attack.

When U. S. reconnaissance patrols reported that the Germans had assembled strong forces to defend Aachen from that direction, General Hodges decided to bypass the city in an encircling maneuver. This entailed coordinated attacks both north and south of the city, with the American pincers clamping shut somewhere east of Aachen. Once he had the city surrounded, Hodges planned to push toward the Rhine River with the bulk of his troops, leaving behind enough men to force the capitulation of Aachen.

This strategy looked good on paper. But no blueprint could foresee the difficulties the Americans faced in carrying out this encirclement. The movement involved the capture of many fortified towns and villages in the populous Aachen region. Moving eastward from the German frontier to a depth of fifteen to twenty-five kilometers, every farmhouse, cottage, barn, and dwelling, every hamlet, town, and village had been incorporated into the Siegfried line. Roads and fields were mined. Barbed wire, antitank ditches, dragon teeth, and machine-gun nests guarded every path. Concrete pillboxes and hidden artillery emplacements protected every mile.

General Hodges' plan meant that these obstacles had to be singly captured or demolished. It also meant that the steep and rocky ridges that dominated the terrain would have to be stormed. The First Army commander realized the task was not an easy one, but he preferred it to a frontal assault on Aachen, where the enemy was strongest. General Hodges believed the Germans were unable to man the Siegfried line and defend each position. He intended to hit hard until a weak spot showed and then to break through with armor and infantry.

Though the offensive had been scheduled for September 11, it was delayed two days for lack of ammunition and rations. At last, at 0800 (8:00 A.M.) on Wednesday, September 13, 1944, General Hodges ordered the VII Corps to attack. General J. Lawton Collins, the corps commander, chose the 1st Division to lead the onslaught.

The shock troop for the attack was Red (1st) Battalion, 16th Infantry Regiment, with White (2nd) Battalion and Blue (3rd) Battalion in reserve. Sherman tanks from the 3rd Armored Division were moved up to support a thrust aimed at a town called Rotgen, two miles inside Germany and four miles southeast of Aachen.

Rotgen had been chosen as the objective because Intelligence reported it lightly held by the Germans. The town, with a population numbering 2,300, was surrounded by several smaller villages which the 16th Regiment would also capture. Rotgen was only one of the many doors that had to be opened before Aachen could be entered.

Lieutenant Colonel Edmund Driscoll, Red Battalion's CO, met for a briefing session with his company commanders and platoon leaders in the battalion command post (CP), a wrecked farmhouse a few yards from the German border. Able (A) Company was picked to lead the assault.

As the conference in the farmhouse was ending, Colonel Driscoll said, "Every man will get hot chow tonight. I won't send our boys in without a good hot dinner."

"But, sir, we can't feed the outposts. They're right up near the Germans," a young lieutenant said.

"Every man gets fed, Lieutenant. Every man. I don't care if he's close enough for a Kraut to share his meal." Driscoll grinned.

That night must have seemed endless to the green replacements in Red Battalion. Only a few days earlier they had been snug in a "Repple Depple" (Replacement Depot) trading pin-up pictures (one Betty Grable was worth two Rita Hayworths and three Marie Wilsons). Then they had not the least care in the world; now they were crouching in foxholes among some of the toughest fighting men in the U. S. Army.

A twenty-year-old platoon sergeant who had been with the division since North Africa made an inspection of his men, checking weapons and equipment. He had five badly shaken rookies in his group.

"Listen to me, you guys," he told them. "Don't be ashamed if you're scared. So am I, so is everybody else, and so are the Krauts. Tomorrow try to obey orders, keep low, and move fast. With luck, you'll make it. If not—" the sergeant shrugged, "if not—well, a man can't live forever."

He could tell them nothing more; he had given a hardened veteran's advice to these untried men. Now each had to fight his own war terrors. In GI talk, every man had to "sweat it out" for himself.

Hot chow was hauled to the front. Sometimes the food bearers came under fire from the enemy. "I didn't mind the bullets," a mess sergeant recalled; "I was worried that the Krauts might hit my coffee vat."

Somehow the food was served and eaten. There was nothing left but to await daylight. At about 2400 (midnight) rain started falling—a nasty rain that was an extra burden of misery. The weather was unchanged at daybreak, September 13, except that it was raining much harder. Sleepy, grouchy GIs climbed out of their foxholes and watched four Sherman tanks from the 3rd Armored clank up to Able Company's CP. One tank had the name DOGHOUSE neatly lettered across its nose.

Twenty-one-year-old First Lieutenant Frank Kolb had the distinction of leading the jump-off platoon. At 0800, Doghouse received the signal, and Kolb's men moved out behind the tank as a barrage was opened by the 105-mm guns of the 5th Field Artillery Battalion. Farther to the rear, VII Corps Long Toms added their roar to the din.

Soon the tank and the soldiers crossed the frontier and were inside Germany. The actual invasion of Hitler's Third Reich had begun. Although shells had destroyed Bildchen three days earlier on September 10, Kolb's men were the first American soldiers to set foot on German ground.

About the time Lieutenant Kolb's platoon splashed forward in the tank's wake, U. S. forces launched a general offensive along every mile of the Westwall from Holland to Switzerland.

Kolb's platoon advanced cautiously. The GIs were wary of German ambushes at every stone wall and wooded patch. Doghouse waddled ahead like a sheep dog. Its cannon swung to cover one potential target after another —but the gunners found nothing to shoot at. Not even a German sniper showed himself and the forward movement seemed more like a training-camp maneuver than real combat.

The Americans moved at a crouch with rifles ready. The soldiers were pale, tensely wide-eyed. Some chewed gum, others had cigarettes dangling from their lips; no one spoke as the men went on like prudent robots.

Somewhere ahead, beyond a green slope, artillery shells were bursting. The rain muffled the explosions, which sounded like distant drums. At last the tank paused on the slope's crest. Gesturing to his platoon to hit the dirt, Kolb crawled to the hilltop where he lay flat, peering through his binoculars.

After several moments, he waved the men on and the GIs crept up to form a firing line. They stared down into the pleasant valley below.

A short distance away they saw Rotgen, a town of neatly clustered houses, surrounded by ridges. It was almost hidden by the misty rain, the smoke of burning buildings, and exploding shells.

Directly beneath the GIs stood the first fortifications of the Siegfried line: five rows of gleaming concrete blocks arrayed in uneven shapes and heights. They had been placed close enough together to block a tank and expose it to the fire of antitank guns concealed on the slopes beyond the town.

"Dragon teeth!" whispered a soldier.

Nobody made jokes now about a dentist yanking the teeth. The open fields in front of the dragon teeth were surely mined and could be swept by machine guns from pillboxes concealed in the dense undergrowth.

Lieutenant Kolb beckoned to his walkie-talkie radioman. He took the instrument and spoke into it, calling for a concentration of artillery fire on the obstacles. Within seconds, the area was blanketed by shell bursts. Even on the slope the earth shook under the impact of the blasting.

When the barrage ceased, Kolb ordered his men forward. They raced down the slope expecting to be met by deadly fire; but only weak and sporadic volleys came from the German pillboxes. As though on a training exercise, the Americans took one strongpoint after another. Engineers cleared the minefields and blew gaps in the dragon teeth with TNT. Tanks and infantry rushed through the breaches, with self-propelled guns (SPG's) following like a torrent of sea water through a broken dike.

"We were luckier than some other divisions," wrote a 1st Division historian. "The VII Corps had moved so rapidly that the enemy did not have time to man all his Westwall defenses in our sector. Most of his defenders were either dead west of Mons or in our PW cages. We had struck a soft spot and thought, in our relief, that we were through the whole Siegfried line. . . ."

36

"This is a cinch," panted an infantryman. "The Krauts are washed up."

He would learn differently, very soon, and keep on learning for weeks to come. . . .

With Kolb's men leading, Able Company swept into Rotgen against feeble resistance. In the town, the GIs found bed sheets, towels, pillowcases—anything white to indicate surrender—hanging from every window.

The victory-flushed Americans deployed in the town square, staring curiously at the first captured German town. Soon enemy civilians appeared, to gaze with equal wonder at the invaders.

Among the Germans was a blond twelve-year-old girl whose neatly braided pigtails hung down her back. She timidly approached a machine-gun-carrying jeep and curtsied to the men in the vehicle.

"*Bitte*. Please. *Bitte*. A favor would you me do?" she said in English with a heavy German accent.

"What's up, sis?" the jeep driver asked.

"*Ach*. In school, English I learn. But well I speak it not. *Bitte*. You will better English help me learn to speak?" she said, pleading with her eyes.

The driver laughed. "Shucks, sis, I don't believe I'll have time to give you lessons."

Late that afternoon all civilians in Rotgen were rounded up and led to the square before the *Burghof* (town hall) where an officer in the 1st Division's Military Police Detachment addressed the crowd.

The officer told the glum Rotgeners that they were now under the jurisdiction of the Allied Military Government

(AMG) and would have to obey the strict regulations imposed by the AMG.

Among the military government edicts were:

A curfew between the hours of 2100 (9:00 P.M.) and 0600 (6:00 A.M.). Unauthorized persons on the street during the forbidden period would be shot. Doctors, nurses, midwives, and priests were issued passes permitting them to be out of doors after curfew.

All firearms, binoculars, and cameras were to be surrendered—possession of any firearm by a German civilian was punishable by death.

Except in churches, gatherings of more than five persons were forbidden.

Newspapers, posters, German or Nazi flags, and patriotic music were banned.

All Nazi officials were subject to arrest.

Any German soldier in civilian clothes would be shot as a spy.

Schools would remain closed until further notice.

The officer concluded with General Dwight D. Eisenhower's forceful declaration and reassurance to the German people: "We come as conquerors but not oppressors!"

The Rotgeners sullenly submitted to the Americans that same day, but a 16th Infantry Red Battalion company had overrun a village called Wallendorf less than a kilometer from Rotgen. There, hard-core Nazi civilians armed with Schmeisser pistols had opened fire from an attic hiding place on the first Yanks to enter Wallendorf. The GIs soon spotted the snipers and silenced them with hand grenades.

The Americans could not permit this to go unpunished. The village had to pay for such resistance.

"If we had let it pass, every Nazi in Germany would've been on our backs. We had to show them we weren't softies. We had to think tough and act mean," an officer said.

The GIs herded the Wallendorfers into the street and then burned the village to the ground as the inhabitants looked on.

"How can you be so cruel?" a housewife cried.

"It's easy, lady," a soldier said. "I only have to remember what you people did in France, Belgium, Norway, Holland, Poland, Russia, and Czechoslovakia. Believe me, lady, it's not hard to be cruel to you Germans. It's not hard at all."

5. IN THE ENEMY'S COUNTRY

GERMANY
September, 1944

SPOTLIGHT ON AACHEN

CHAPTER 5

SUMMER WAS ENDING, its promises drowned in the mud before Aachen. It rained steadily every day after September 13. Dirt roads became bogs. Trucks, jeeps, and SPG's wallowed in fields turned to quagmire and swamps. Tanks were trapped in meadowland marshes. Soldiers struggled through knee-deep mud.

Cold winds drove the rain. Fog closed in. Overhead arched a slate-gray sky. The days passed from dreary dawn to brooding night.

The weather which plagued the continent of Europe during the last half of September closed all airfields, and the U. S. Army Air Corps was grounded. Infantrymen living in unrelieved discomfort no longer could look up at bombers and fighters speeding on to pound German roads, railway tracks, factories, and supply dumps.

At Aachen, the war was stalled by mud and rain. The slashing U. S. offensive so optimistically launched on September 13 became a vicious struggle amidst the maze of barbed wire and concrete that was the Siegfried line.

The Americans lost men for every foot of the Westwall, yet did not flinch. Every day, the Yanks eked out some gains along the front. But where only weeks before advances had been measured in miles, by mid-September, a day's sacrifices in blood and equipment totaled a forward movement of only a few yards.

To the GIs, the Siegfried line was a particular hell especially reserved for foot soldiers. They sloshed across shell-torn pasture lands into the dragon teeth, land mines, booby traps, and pillboxes.

"What a war," a GI lamented. "If booby traps and land mines don't get you, burp guns will. But the cards are stacked so even that if you survive the Siegfried line you'll wind up with trench-rot, frostbite, influenza, pneumonia, or the shakes. What a war!"

American casualties rose steeply. Figures for a five-day period (Friday, September 15—Wednesday, September 20) showed that Red Battalion, 16th Infantry, had suffered losses amounting to 300 killed, wounded, or missing out of its 1,300-man total strength.

Despite every hardship, the 1st Division and the other American divisions on the German frontier kept slugging away at the enemy. In less than a week the 1st Division captured a dozen German towns and villages and stabbed deeply into the Siegfried line.

The Americans confronted difficult problems after taking a German town. The GIs were now well inside Germany, surrounded by a hostile populace. Facing unfriendly civilians was a new experience for the Yanks. Before, people had greeted them with open arms. In France and Belgium, which the Nazis had occupied, the Americans had been showered with flowers, kisses, and wine; the crowds there had hailed them as liberators. Every hand was outstretched in welcome to the Americans and turned against the Germans.

Inside Germany it was different. Every window, every doorway might shield a sniper. The pretty girls with blue eyes and straw-colored hair might be members of the Hitler Jugend (Hitler Youth) hiding hand grenades in their shopping baskets. The middle-aged burgher at the roadside might be a Nazi official or an SS officer in disguise. In Germany, the GIs found no friendly faces and heard no laughter; they moved in an atmosphere of suspicion and distrust.

Danger from German civilians was real enough.

Three military policemen were kidnaped in Rotgen and beaten up by a gang of German teen-agers. At various places, snipers fired at GIs, and at least one sentry was stabbed to death. The Nazi "underground" had begun striking at the Americans. However, not every German openly displayed hostility to them. Many who spoke

English tried to ingratiate themselves with the invaders.

A shopkeeper in Walheim, a little town north of Rotgen, cornered a GI and confided, "I am glad you have come. The Americans are welcome. Never would I harm an American. I have a brother in your country. He lives in Wisconsin. Please, can you give me a good American cigarette?"

"I figured you were trying to con me," the soldier said. "No cigarette!" He pushed past the German and moved on.

"*Verdammt Amerikaner!*" the shopkeeper was heard to mutter. "Damned American!"

It seemed to the Americans that rooting out the Nazis was not going to be simple. But this was not so in one captured town south of Aachen where the AMG (Allied Military Government) personnel came in on the heels of the tanks and infantry that had taken the place. Even while gunfire was still rattling in some parts of the town, the AMG CO (Commanding Officer) ordered all civilians to gather outside the town hall.

The inhabitants responded and formed a long single line when so ordered. The officer then asked each individual in precise German, "Are you a Nazi party member? When did you join?"

One after another came the answers. "I am not a Nazi, sir. I never have been."

After a score of negative replies, the officer lost his temper. Slamming his helmet on the ground, he cried, "You're lying! Damn it! Some of you must have belonged to the party! Where in blazes are all the Nazis?"

An AMG sergeant stepped up to the irate captain. "Sir, I'd like to take a crack at this crowd."

"Go ahead, Sergeant! Go ahead! I can't get to first base with them," the officer said.

The sergeant faced the Germans who were looking on with amused contempt. In German, the noncom bawled: *"Achtung!"* His voice rang with authority. The crowd stiffened to attention.

"Heil Hitler!" bellowed the sergeant, thrusting his arm out in the Nazi salute.

Years of conditioning and training brought instant reaction. Several hundred hands shot up in a similar gesture.

"You will now tell the truth," the sergeant declared. "You have just shown us that you are Nazis. Anyone who lies will be shot as an example to the rest. Do you understand?"

"Ja!" the people cried in unison.

"Good! Now, all those who joined the party before 1933, move one pace to the left. Those who joined after 1933, move one pace to the right. Nonparty people stay where you are. Now—move!" the sergeant roared.

The townspeople responded to his commands. Some stepped to the left, more went to the right, and a handful remained in place. The sergeant grinned at the AMG captain.

"Mission accomplished, sir," he said. "All you have to do is count 'em."

"I don't get it, Sergeant," the captain said, shaking his head. "I treated them so nicely—and you—"

"Don't try to figure out Germans, sir. I only know my way works. They want things done like that." The sergeant smiled.

Although the Americans found many German civilians bitterly outspoken about the turn in the war, their own plight, the bombings and the shellings, only a few denounced Hitler or the Nazis. An outstanding exception to this occurred in a village named Rott where the local Nazi leader of the Storm Troopers (SA) tried to flee on a bicycle while still wearing his Nazi uniform. He was spotted by two American MP's in a jeep as he pedaled away.

The Americans overtook the fleeing man and brought him back to the village where the jeep was surrounded by a crowd of local citizens. A woman leaped forward and berated the Nazi official.

"*Schweinhund!*" she screamed. "Swine! Dog! Murderer! She spat in his face and went for him, clawing and scratching. With difficulty, the MP's pulled her off the cringing man.

"Why did you treat him like that?" a German-speaking MP asked. "Don't you like the Nazis?"

"I hate the Nazi dogs! They are dragging Germany down into ruins. We are losing the war!" the woman cried.

"And how did you feel about Nazis when Germany was winning?" the MP said.

"Ach, then it was different. Then they were *wunderbar*—wonderful!" the woman beamed.

To avoid incidents with German civilians, all U. S.

personnel were ordered not to show any friendliness to Germans. No soldier was to drive or visit with a German or to buy local goods. GIs were forbidden to go sightseeing in captured towns and cities. Conversation with Germans, except in the line of duty was also prohibited. Violators of these rules were subject to fines and punishment.

However, the decrees were difficult to enforce. Many GIs willingly risked court martial to flirt with pretty *Fräuleins*. No authority could stop a kindly soldier from passing a few cigarettes to an old man, or giving a can of rations to a hungry waif.

However, while the GIs flouted their own regulations, embittered Nazis did not soften toward the invaders. A civilian in conquered German territory who cooperated with the Americans imperiled his life.

The Nazi Minister of Propaganda, Joseph Goebbels, warned: ". . . in occupied German districts there will be no German civil administration, no German executive bodies, no German courts. No functionary will follow the enemy orders . . . without the certainty that soon . . . he will be crucified in his own window!"

Goebbels' threats were not empty ones. Nazi fanatics resurrected a medieval Teutonic institution—the Feme, or punishment court—which centuries before had dealt with German traitors. The Feme, a secret organization, resembled the Mafia or the Ku Klux Klan. Members of the Feme, cloaked, hooded, and masked, hunted down, kidnaped, and executed all those they deemed "traitors." Germans who helped the Americans bring order to occupied areas lived in constant dread of capture by the Feme, which always passed the death sentence on its victims.

U. S. counterintelligence agents finally wiped out the Feme in the Aachen region, but not until a number of militant anti-Nazi Germans had been murdered in cold blood by assassins.

Other secret Nazi societies tried to disrupt the American occupation with behind-the-lines sabotage, assassination, and terror. The most prominent of these groups was the terror band known as Werwolf (Werewolf). Its ranks were filled by teen-age boys and girls. These young people had been taught to believe there was no greater glory than to die for the Fuehrer. The members of Werwolf took a ritualistic blood oath to fight the enemy. "He who dies for Hitler shall live forever in German hearts!" the deluded youths chanted.

It was one thing to make such a dramatic vow, and something else to carry it out. The idea of dying for Hitler really did not enchant the young Nazis. Life, even under the Americans, was far sweeter than death. Very few of them ever struck a blow at the Americans. Even the acts they did commit, ineffectual sniping and inept attempts at sabotage, were little more than nuisances to the Yanks. The Werewolves and other German "patriots" limited their defiance mainly to glaring at the Americans and muttering curses behind the GIs' backs. U. S. agents quickly broke up the Werwolf, which had proved to have more growl than bite.

While Nazi civilian resistance was slight in the rear

areas, military opposition to the Americans at the front grew more formidable daily. The Americans were discomfited to find that after all the terrible fighting in the mud and rain they had not yet pierced the main part of the Siegfried line. The pillboxes, bunkers, and blockhouses blasted by U. S. artillery and overrun by infantry were auxiliary positions that ran south of Aachen, not in the real line.

First Division patrols discovered that the actual Siegfried line began at Stolberg, an industrial city five miles southeast of Aachen and about that far from the Belgian frontier. A 3rd Armored Division task force and elements of Red Battalion, 16th Infantry, probed the defenses around Stolberg. A report from a scouting party succinctly said, "It's going to be rugged. The Krauts are rough in this sector."

As these moves were being made against Stolberg, the U. S. 30th Infantry Division, XIX Corps, farther north, started to build up for a drive in a southerly direction through the Siegfried line to link up with the 1st Division, which was driving northward. Somewhere east of Aachen, it was hoped that the two American divisions would meet.

On Thursday, September 14, the 3rd Armored task force had broken the German fortifications at Münsterbusch on the Stolberg road and the advantage was exploited by Red Battalion, 16th Infantry, which promptly charged into Münsterbusch where a hot battle raged as the Germans fought doggedly for every position.

General Clarence Huebner (CO, 1st Division) reinforced Red Battalion with White and Blue Battalions, 16th Infantry, and the 3rd Armored Division rushed more tanks into the fray. For two days the fighting roared on without pause. By nightfall, Saturday, September 16, the GIs had made decided progress toward Stolberg. Red and White Battalions had captured important high ground overlooking the city and the Yanks dug in to consolidate their gains.

Bone-tired Americans ate cold C rations and tried to get some sleep in their flooded foxholes. Despite the discomfort, the GIs were not discontented. They had done well during the past forty-eight hours. The roads southeast of Aachen had been cut, and an exit from the city was no longer possible in that direction. The first steps to surround and isolate Aachen had been successfully concluded.

About five miles northwest of Stolberg, where Aachen's outskirts touched the border of Holland, the 30th "Old Hickory" Division slashed the Maastricht-Heerlen-Aachen road and elements of the division had seized high ground on the west slope of the Wurm River in the vicinity of Heerlen. The 30th Division got ready to cross the Wurm and clear out the Germans in the northern and northeastern sectors around Aachen, but the rain so hampered this operation that little progress was made.

The unrelenting wet weather created many problems for the Americans. Besides grounding the Air Corps, it brought on another supply shortage. The steady rainfall slowed traffic on the Red Ball Line. Roads leading from the west oozed with mud. Swollen streams weakened and washed out bridges so that long detours were necessary. The huge trucks of the Red Ball Line could no longer roll through the night at top speed. They were often forced to crawl for miles in low gear on flooded roadways. Too often, overladen trailers floundered hubcap deep in mud, blocking other convoys until cursing, sweating drivers dug out their vehicles after hours of back-breaking labor.

As supply deliveries were delayed, the GIs at the front once again felt the pinch. Artillery shells were limited; even rifle ammunition was curtailed, and forward units had nothing to eat but their emergency D rations.

The fighting assumed a nightmarish quality. The fog cut down visibility so drastically that a reconnaissance sergeant from the 113th Armored Cavalry Battalion, returning from a patrol in his light, half-track scout car, reported to his CO: "Don't ask me what's out there, sir. I couldn't tell you. They should have sent a seeing-eye dog."

While the weather also trammeled the Germans, it gave them a specific advantage. Since they knew the terrain, the enemy was able to move in the fog without much trouble. Because American planes were grounded, the Germans had almost complete freedom to move reinforcements up into the Siegfried line. Nor did the Germans lack ammunition. Years before, when the war began, Hitler had ordered tons of ammunition buried in concrete vaults placed around Aachen, as if he had foreseen that one day the Germans might have to make a desperate stand there. Millions of bullets, thousands of artillery shells, and tremendous stocks of hand grenades were available to Aachen's defenders. Thanks to Hitler's intuitions, the Wehrmacht had the ammunition it needed to fight the invaders.

The tired, bedraggled GIs entrenched atop the ridges near Stolberg did not know this. They believed that sooner or later the Germans would run short of ammunition. But they soon discovered that this was only wishful thinking.

At 0400 (4:00 A.M.), Sunday, September 17, Red and White Battalions, 16th Infantry, were warned that forward listening posts had reported large-scale movement of enemy troops and tanks in Stolberg. Undoubtedly the Germans were readying a counterattack. The GIs were rousted out of their foxholes and set to work digging additional emplacements. The wet dirt flew as they hacked out new positions. Daylight was breaking when a muddy, drenched soldier flung a shovelful of mud over his shoulder and paused for a moment.

"Join the army and learn a trade!" he sneered. "Ditch diggers, that's what we are. Ditch diggers!"

"Aw, quit your bellyachin'," another soldier said. "It's healthy outdoor work, isn't it?"

6. IN CRUCIAL BATTLE

STOLBERG, GERMANY
Sunday, September 17, 1944—
Sunday, September 24, 1944

THE FIGHT FOR STOLBERG

CHAPTER 6

Red and white battalions, 16th Infantry, waited in the rain for the Germans. Sometime after daylight, Blue (3rd) Battalion, 18th Infantry, crept up from the 1st Division reserve to reinforce them.

Among the new arrivals was Sergeant Walter D. Ehlers, Love (L) Company, a squad leader. Ehlers checked his men and, after making sure his machine-gun section was set to sweep the treeless ridge face, wrapped himself in his poncho and went to sleep in the rain. Not everyone on the slope possessed Ehlers' calmness. Each man had to prepare himself in his own way for what was coming. Some hid their fears in a flow of talk, jokes, and wisecracks. Others crouched in moody silence, perhaps remembering a time when being out in the rainy dawn meant nothing more exciting than a camping trip. Perhaps the men wondered if they would survive that day, the next, and the one after that and someday go home to jobs, school, wives, sweethearts, families, and friendly places.

In one foxhole, a machine-gun crew discussed the coming World Series between the St. Louis Browns and the St. Louis Cardinals. In another, an argument broke out about the American presidential election to be held in November. That year Franklin D. Roosevelt, running for his fourth term, was opposed by Thomas Dewey.

A bespectacled rifleman lectured his squad on what should be done with Germany when the Nazis were defeated. "Knock it off!" his squad leader growled. "The war's not over yet. We still have to lick the Nazis and that'll take some doing!"

Ammunition bearers slid down the rear slope of the ridge to the battalion supply dump and toiled back up the slippery trail lugging boxes of rifle and machine-gun bullets. Company cooks hauled hot coffee to the firing line. As the darkness faded, the soldiers stared hard through the rain and fog for a glimpse of the enemy. The front was so quiet that they could hear the clattering of mess kits and canteen cups.

For minutes at a time no shot was fired in that whole sector. The silence added to the tension. The gray fog hung more thickly than ever in a dense, slowly swirling veil that enwrapped the men like a huge shroud.

58

The GIs fidgeted nervously. Machine guns and rifles were checked a dozen times and then a dozen times more. Cigarettes were tiny red eyes glowing in the opaque dawn. Someone cleared his throat, and the sound reverberated in that uncanny stillness.

An officer glanced at his wrist watch. "Hello, Red Dog One. It's oh six hundred (6:00 A.M.)," he whispered into the field telephone that connected him to a forward outpost. "Keep your eyes peeled."

"Danger Red! Danger Red!" the outpost (OP) replied. "This is Red Dog One! I hear tanks to my immediate front. Don't see them yet."

"Find them, Red Dog One!" the officer replied.

"I see them now!" There was a slight pause. "Holy Cow! Here they come! Straight at me! Six Tigers! What are my orders?"

"Orders! Move out, you jerk!" the officer cried, forgetting all military procedure.

At 0601 (6:01 A.M.) every man on the ridge heard the tanks clanking in the distance. "Oh, brother. We've bought it," a rifleman muttered.

The giant German Mark VI (Tiger) tanks ground through the mud, skidding and swaying when their caterpillar treads lost traction in the slimy ground. As they advanced, German batteries opened against the ridge. The earth heaved under the blasting of the 88-mm shells. Geysers of dirt and stone showered the GIs. Shrapnel zinged through the rain.

"Medic! Medic!" a wounded man shrieked.

The battle was on.

Quite unexpectedly, a brisk wind dispelled the fog. The Yanks, ducking under the pitiless cannonading, could see the line of tanks waddling toward them across the barren open ground that stretched out from Stolberg to the foot of the ridge. Behind the armored machines trotted rows of widely dispersed German infantry. From that distance the enemy troops looked like toys.

An American artillery liaison officer studied the scene through his binoculars for a moment and then picked up the hand phone that linked him to a section of 105-mm guns. The code for that battery happened to be Darling.

"Darling," the officer cooed into the mouthpiece. "I have a lovely target for you." He gave the range and waited.

About twenty seconds later, exploding shells blossomed around the tanks. "Darling," the officer murmured, "you're almost on the button. Up one-five-zero and right five-zero and you'll hit pay dirt."

A Tiger tank shuddered under a direct hit. Black smoke vomited from its turret. A second tank stopped dead as a shell blast knocked off its treads. The hatch cover flew open, and tiny crewmen tumbled out to disappear in the smoke and flame of more shell bursts. The remaining four tanks swept on. GIs with bazookas popped out of foxholes, and the blast of HE projectiles rocked the big tanks. A gun turret was demolished, and sheets of fire poured from the Tiger. The surviving German armor slid about in wide circles and pulled back out of range.

On rushed the German infantry, charging forward in skirmish formation—a squad dashed ahead and then hit the ground as another group leap-frogged over them. Not even the American artillery could stop the Germans, and they reached the slope, scrambling uphill, slipping in the mud, rising again. The German artillery fell silent and the American 105-mm gunners, fearing to hit their own men, also ceased firing.

Then, all along the ridge line, machine guns and rifles opened up. In the face of those fierce volleys the Germans struggled to the crest. These Germans were no bottom-of-the-barrel troops scraped together for a last-ditch attack. They were splendidly trained and disciplined soldiers hardened by years of combat.

American small arms fire reached a furious peak. The advancing Germans, taking advantage of any cover they found, fought back with light machine guns, Schmeisser pistols, and small-bore mortars.

Soon the enemy was only fifty yards away and the Yanks could see the SS death's-head shoulder patches on the battle jackets of the advancing Germans. Now the GIs knew they were facing the foe's best fighting men. The American line stood firm. There was no wavering even when the command "Fix bayonets!" was passed along.

As the SS men came closer, the *whump, whump* of exploding hand grenades was added to the din of battle. The Nazis ran forward, screaming, "Heil, Hitler!" They scrambled on over the crest of the ridge and swarmed into the American perimeter. GIs climbed out of their

61

foxholes to grapple with the enemy. Men wrestled in the mud. Shrieking soldiers, transfixed by bayonets, writhed in agony. The foes fought with fists, knives, and clubbed rifles until the outnumbered SS broke and ran, fleeing pell-mell downhill as bullets kicked up spurts of mud at their heels.

But not all the attackers ran.

One tall German stood his ground. His helmet was gone and his fine blond hair matted his forehead like a net of yellow silk. He kept charging forward, running clumsily in the mud, firing his burp gun until the magazine was empty. Even then, he was not through. He dropped the gun and whipped out a trench knife which he brandished over his head.

He was the only survivor of his platoon; comrades lay sprawled dead and wounded in heaps about him. A GI recalled that lone man's stand: "This German must have gone mad. I remember how the guys around me stopped shooting and gawked at him like they would at a freak. Then one of our boys belted him in the chest with his rifle butt. The Nazi sort of deflated like a punctured balloon. He dropped slowly to the ground in a sitting position. He looked around at us glassy-eyed, put his face in his hands, and bawled like a seven-year-old kid."

An SS captain was captured on the ridge and, while waiting to board a truck back to the POW compound, he cried out in English: "I was three years in Russia! I escaped at Stalingrad! Now, to be taken like this in my own country. I shall never live down the disgrace. Shoot me! Shoot me!"

"It's not that bad, Fritzie, get into the truck," a grizzled GI said.

The SS captain drew himself stiffly erect and folded his arms across his chest. "Never! I prefer death to a prisoner-of-war cage."

"Okay, pal," the American said. "If you're not aboard by the time I count three—" He raised his M-1 rifle and aimed it at the German's head.

The officer's eyes widened in horror. "You'd shoot me in cold blood?"

"Just trying to oblige." The Yank's finger tightened on the trigger. "One—, two—"

The German let out a horrified cry and clambered into the truck, which pulled out at once with its load of prisoners. The GI leaned on his rifle and scratched his three-day stubble of beard.

"Those Krauts beat me," he said. "All that bunk about us shooting him. I knew he was only batting his gums. When a man really wants to die he doesn't bleat about it. He gets himself killed. It's not hard to do out here."

"They think it's an honor to die for Hitler," another soldier said.

The first GI shrugged. "What's the point? The way I see it, a man ought to live for his country."

The determined attack on the U. S. ridge positions had been made by two battalions of the 27th SS Waffen (Combat) Regiment, one of Germany's finest fighting units. One battalion was nearly decimated in the wild charge. Baker (B) Company, 16th Infantry, counted 250 dead Germans in front of its position. Some of them had fallen thirty to forty yards inside the American positions.

The 27th SS hurled two more attacks against the Americans, but these assaults lacked power, and the Yanks on the ridge held fast. By 1100 (11:00 A.M.) the last SS had trudged back into the Siegfried line. An American counterattack was swiftly mounted. Medium and heavy U. S. 3rd Armored Division tanks rolled up to open the Stolberg road.

This tank column, commanded by Lieutenant Colonel Sam Hogan, a Texan, was called "Task Force Hogan" after its CO. Colonel Hogan's armor raced straight down the well-defended approaches to Stolberg. The 3rd Division task force was opposed by elements of the 9th Panzer (Armored) Division, which had lost its vehicles and was fighting as infantry.

Sam Hogan had the dashing temperament of a Civil War cavalry commander. He was a twentieth-century version of Jeb Stuart, Nathan B. Forrest, and George Custer rolled into one. Daring, but never reckless, Hogan sent his tanks in flashing raids on the German positions. The enemy never knew where the American vehicles might next appear, either to blast a road block or to shoot up a machine-gun position.

"What we did was keep the Krauts off balance. We'd send a few tanks to tweak their noses and another column to kick them in the pants. They were a pretty confused bunch by the time we were finished with them," a Task Force Hogan tank driver reminisced.

Closely following the tanks came the 16th Infantry

Regiment in trucks, jeeps, weapons carriers, and on foot. Squads of GIs rode atop Hogan's tanks. They roared down the highway yelling "On to Stolberg!"

The bedeviled Germans tried hard to stop the push, but the GIs pounded them with 81-mm mortars and 105-mm cannon until no square foot around Stolberg was free of shell holes. Despite huge losses, the 9th Panzer Division finally managed to slow, but not stem, the American attack.

By Saturday, September 23, the Yanks had pushed shock troops through the Siegfried line, which guarded the city, and fighting flared in Stolberg's streets. The GIs had improvised ways to knock out the Siegfried line's pillboxes. Instead of risking men in frontal assaults, the GIs used bulldozers to shove mounds of earth atop the doors and firing slits of the pillboxes. The Germans could either surrender or suffocate in the airtight bunkers.

They also used more conventional methods of taking strongpoints. Demolition teams moved up under a smoke-shell barrage to plant TNT charges at the doors of the pillboxes. The blasts welded the doors shut and trapped the enemy inside. The Americans also employed flame throwers, satchel charges, and bangalore torpedoes. The latter were long poles with a package of high explosive attached to one end. They were thrust into the pillbox through a firing slit and the charge detonated, to stun or kill those within the emplacement.

After almost a week of this grim fighting, the 16th Infantry Regiment was once more reinforced by Blue Battalion, 18th Infantry. The added weight of the fresh troops drove the Germans back into the center of Stolberg. There the enemy entrenched so strongly that every effort to dislodge him by direct assault failed.

The 18th Infantry CO decided to use trickery on the Germans. He ordered Sergeant Walter Ehlers, who was a veteran of North Africa and Normandy and had won both the Silver Star and the Bronze Star, to infiltrate the enemy position and, if possible, work his way with a squad to the center of Stolberg. He was to create a distraction inside the town while strong American units attacked the enemy frontally during the confusion Ehlers had caused.

After dark on Saturday, September 23, Ehlers sneaked his Love Company squad past several German strongpoints and slipped into Stolberg where his men hid themselves in a ruined house that faced the main square. The GIs lay silent all night long in the midst of the German positions. The slightest noise would have betrayed their presence.

It rained all that Saturday night and was still raining at daybreak, Sunday, when four Mark VI (Tiger) tanks clashed and clattered into Stolberg from the east, the treads making an awesome racket on the centuries-old cobblestones. The tanks parked close together in the square. Hatches clanged open as the crews poked out their heads for fresh air.

Sergeant Ehlers motioned to his bazooka man. The rocket launcher was raised. A tongue of fire stabbed from its mouth and the wet morning was torn by an explosion. Every man in Ehlers' squad reared up, to blaze away with his rifle or lob hand grenades into the open tank turrets.

Oily smoke enshrouded the tanks. The huge vehicles were torn by internal explosions. Flames belched from the gutted insides and crew men reeled to the ground, their clothing ablaze. They shrieked like agonized animals. Two German tankers braved the fire to stay atop one of the burning vehicles. They swung a machine gun at the house where Ehlers' squad was hidden.

Tracer bullets streaked at the Americans. Wood splinters flew around them. Ehlers grabbed a rifle and picked off the gunners with well-aimed shots. At that instant two Sherman tanks from Task Force Hogan swung around a corner. The tank cannon began blasting enemy positions around the square. More American armor rolled in and joined the barrage. A company from the 16th Infantry worked through the streets behind the enemy strongholds. Grenades exploded and bazookas *swooshed*. A section of 81-mm mortars began lobbing shells upon the Germans. Soon white cloths fluttered from windows and cellars. Dust-covered German soldiers, hands raised in surrender, crept out of the ruins. Stolberg was taken.

Later, Sergeant Ehlers sat in a first-aid station while Love Company's aid man bandaged a slight arm wound the noncom had received.

"Golly, Sarge," the medic said, "you really must hate the Germans."

"Why?"

"The way you keep knocking 'em off."

Ehlers shook his head. "You're wrong, pill roller. I

don't hate anybody. And I don't like to kill anybody. But if somebody gets in my way when I have a job to do so I have to kill him so I can get on with it, then I kill him and that's all there is to it."

7. THE DESOLATE LAND

GERMANY

September, 1944

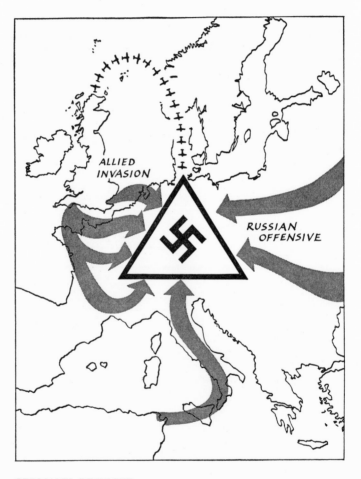

GERMANY BESIEGED

CHAPTER 7

THE MONTH OF September was almost over, and the American failure to capture Aachen gave German morale a tremendous lift. While it was true that the mounting pressures had been too much for some German soldiers to bear, the generally low spirits of the Wehrmacht and the auxiliary Volkssturm had soared. When the American offensive against Germany had started and grave doubts existed that the Siegfried line could be held, only Nazi fanatics did not despair.

U. S. MP's caught Wehrmacht and Volkssturm deserters in every town and village the First Army captured. German soldiers surrendered by the score despite Nazi warnings of reprisals against the families of anyone who gave up. Life in a POW compound seemed preferable to dying for a doomed cause.

Although many Germans felt this, the SS troops never wavered in their loyalty to Hitler. "The only way to take an SS man was to kill him," an American officer said. In some sectors held by SS units, American demolition teams had to blow up a position to drive out the defenders.

During the last week of September, 1944, an unreasonable optimism spread among the Germans. The people who had grown panicky during the swift American advances of July, August, and early September, now took heart and rallied around their Fuehrer. As usual, Hitler had been right, they believed. Was not Aachen standing against the invader like a Teutonic Gilbraltar? Did not the Siegfried line remain unbroken, like a mighty dam holding back the invasion flood?

Because the rainy and foggy weather prevented aerial bombardment of Germany, many wishful thinkers pointed this out as an example of Hitler's invincibility. The Germans were swept by a curious, quasi-religious fervor at what they deemed to be divine intervention on their behalf.

"God must be with us," they exulted, "else why would he give us such bad weather to ground the enemy planes?"

A spate of wild and fanciful rumors blanketed Germany:

England and the United States had turned against Russia to halt the spread of communism; General Eisenhower had been assassinated; the Americans had suffered such huge losses over Germany of planes and men that the U. S. Army Air Corps was crippled; popular antiwar sentiment in the United States would defeat President Roosevelt in the November elections, and Thomas Dewey, Republican candidate, intended to negotiate for peace; the German V-2 rocket offensive was bringing England to her knees.

Those baseless rumors went on and on. Under normal circumstances, no one would have believed such talk— but the times were not normal, and since 1933 the Germans had grown accustomed to accept lies rather than truth. Now they grasped at every rumor, even the most incredible ones, and regarded them as hopeful beacons in the closing darkness.

In September, 1944, a German might have reasoned, "Everything is not yet lost. Our armies are holding. The enemy has not bombed us for almost two weeks. We grow stronger every day."

But not every German was deceived into believing imminent defeat had miraculously become a victory. They dared to point out that only the weather had grounded the American planes. One day, the clouds would lift and the enemy aircraft would again blast Germany. The Siegfried line could not hold out forever; Germany was beaten, whipped, kaput. Such people were labeled as defeatists, and arrested by the Gestapo for treason. That charge was tantamount to a death sentence.

That autumn, all through Germany, it became common to see bodies dangling from trees and lamp posts with a placard reading "Defeatist" pinned to the victim's clothing. By stamping out opposition in this way, Hitler bolstered Germany's determination to fight on, despite the imminent possibility of military collapse.

At the front, too, this policy was applied to the soldiers. Colonel Gerhardt Wilck, the CO of the Aachen garrison, announced that any unit which retreated, unless so ordered by him, would be purged of "weaklings, traitors, and cowards." He amplified this by promising to execute one man out of every ten among troops "that failed to properly serve the Fatherland."

The Aachen commander applied other stringent measures. Every soldier in the city had to swear upon his honor that he would fight until the end. In a special message to the garrison, Wilck declared: "Death is preferable to dishonor. If the Americans should enter Aachen let it be over the bodies of German heroes! Any man who thinks otherwise is a coward and a disgrace to the Fatherland! Heil Hitler!"

However, the Colonel did not depend only on bombast to steel the Wehrmacht troops he commanded. He posted SS men with orders to shoot any Wehrmacht officer or enlisted man who attempted to surrender. This stirred anew the long-standing hatred between Wehrmacht and SS. The average German soldier both feared and envied the men of the Elite Corps. In Hitler's Germany, the SS enjoyed such special privileges as higher pay, better rations, and greater status than the other military units. All these special considerations were given the SS to ensure the unswerving, unquestioned loyalty of every man. The ranks of the SS were filled by young, ardent

Nazis whose devotion to Hitler reached adulation. To them, Hitler was God. His orders were divine commandments.

With such men to ride herd on his soldiers, Wilck felt confident that there would be no defectors in the Aachen garrison. However, the Wehrmacht men defending the city grew more resentful each day over the presence of so many SS troopers. Every fourth soldier in Aachen was an SS man. The Elite Corps men treated the ordinary soldiers with scorn and contempt. The SS behaved so arrogantly that when the chance came during a battle, vengeful Wehrmacht soldiers shot their tormentors in the back.

But despite everything, the average German soldier remained faithful to his duty to the Fatherland. To him, German soil was sacred, not to be violated by an outsider, and, while the soldier knew his country was dying, he still had to keep fighting on a little longer. This he owed to the comrades who had fallen in Poland, France, Norway, Russia, North Africa—in blazing desert and frozen tundra. Never had armies won such victories as had the Germans, but the triumphs were empty ones; the way was strewn with corpses and not flowers.

The German soldier at the front knew of the terrible destruction Allied planes were bringing to the homeland. Cities were leveled and thousands of dead buried under the rubble. Letters from behind the lines told him what was happening.

Soon he began to realize that the longer he resisted, the longer the war would continue and the longer the bombs would rain on Germany. Perhaps no one knew better than he how much the country deserved such retribution. The German soldier had seen unspeakable atrocities, fiendish brutalities, and ghastly horrors committed every place Hitler's legions had violated.

The Wehrmacht was seldom guilty of these crimes. Such work was left to specialists trained in mass murder. But almost every German soldier and many civilians as well had witnessed Hitler's "New Order" in practice—wholesale havoc and mass slaughter. At first the soldiers had been appalled at what was being done. But even decent men soon grew callous to the atrocities. Besides, this sort of thing was necessary, Hitler told them, if the "New Order" was to flourish. As true Germans, they believed him.

But no matter how loyal or patriotic a soldier might be, bad news from home succeeded in crushing him where all the American guns, planes, and tanks had failed. Every letter had a message of despair. The case of one humble German soldier, Corporal Kaspar Gottwald, 352nd Infantry Regiment, was typical of many in the Wehrmacht.

Perhaps Kaspar Gottwald would have been killed fighting from his pillbox near Aachen if he had not received a letter from home. Dated September 9, the letter reached him on September 27. (Front-line mail deliveries were understandably delayed.)

The letter was from his mother. It read:

"Dearest Son:

"How can I tell you? Your beloved wife, Ilse, was

killed in a bombing raid. Your house is gone, too. A direct hit. God spared the children and they are now with me. Kaspar, there is agony all around. Who could have believed this would happen? Had we but known where Hitler was leading us. . . . Oh dear God. . . ."

Kaspar never finished reading. He crumpled the letter into a ball and crushed it in his fist as though to squeeze out the awful message it held.

He told no one about the letter and sat alone, dry-eyed, brooding. He had had enough—too much. He was through. With Ilse gone, the children had no one but him. He had to live for them, and his chances of that grew slimmer each day he stayed on the line.

That night, Corporal Kaspar Gottwald sneaked out of the pillbox and crawled to an American outpost where he surrendered. He was sent back to a CP for questioning.

For a long time Kaspar stood silently under the questioning of a U. S. Intelligence officer. Suddenly he burst into tears.

"What's eating him?" the officer asked the sergeant serving as his interpreter.

The sergeant talked to Kaspar, who finally answered, fighting to control himself.

"Well?" asked the officer.

"I think we ought to ease up on him, sir," the interpreter said. "Our planes killed his wife and he heard about it only this morning. Now he says he must stay alive so he can come back some day and look after his kids. That's why he deserted."

The officer eyed Kaspar for a moment and nodded. "I see. Okay, Sergeant, no more questions. Send him to the rear."

Kaspar Gottwald's war was over.

8. THE BIG PUSH

CROSSING OF THE WURM RIVER, GERMANY
Sunday, October 1, 1944

THE BREAKTHROUGH AT UBACH

CHAPTER 8

Early on the morning of Wednesday, September 27, even as the grueling fighting north and south of Aachen roared on, the 1st Division took time out for a behind-the-lines ceremony.

Just after daybreak fifty officers, noncoms, and privates slogged through the mud to General Huebner's head-quarters, a modest cottage located near a sawmill on the edge of a ravine two or three miles behind the battle lines.

The men had been summoned from their foxholes by their CO to receive medals won for bravery in combat during the D-Day landings on June 6, 1944. No matter how incongruous the situation, army tradition had to be carried out. It had taken weeks for the citations to pass through channels and the awards to be approved by higher headquarters.

Chilling rain swept across the slope as the fifty men arrayed themselves in two lines and waited. At 0700 (7:00 A.M.) staff cars drew up to the cottage. Out stepped General Courtney H. Hodges, the First Army CO, followed by General J. Lawton Collins, the VII Corps CO. Huebner greeted his superiors, and after a brief conversation, the three generals, attended by their staffs, approached the men drawn up in the ranks. The fifty soldiers stiffened to attention.

The citations were read. After each recitation, General Huebner pinned the appropriate medal on each man's mud-stained field jacket. The three generals solemnly saluted the medal winners and shook hands with them. The brief ceremony soon ended without further pomp. The fifty soldiers slopped back to their separate units and the day's fighting.

The men were little impressed by their decorations. One combat-weary sergeant glanced at the glittering Silver Star dangling from his jacket. "That's exactly what I needed. Now the Krauts will know I'm a hero and drop dead when they see me," he commented wryly.

The ceremony had been a melancholy affair. Such occasions were meant to take place on green parade grounds in dazzling sunlight with bands blaring, flags fluttering, and crowds looking on. Instead, as one eyewitness observed, "The only music was the whistling of the chill damp wind sweeping over meadows which only a few days before had been German soil. . . ."

Although the medal winners disparaged the deeds for which the decorations had been awarded, they were truly heroes. One was a gentle-voiced staff sergeant from Virginia who had never missed a day's action with the division even when wounded. On D-Day he had single-handedly knocked out two German machine guns.

Another soldier had been the only surviving noncom in his section. He organized five attacks on a German position until it was finally captured, and all without orders or guidance from any superior. The ceremony's observer further said, "I prayed that all of those brave boys would survive the coming battles and the war; but in my heart I doubted it. Such men cannot be lucky all the time."

In fact, luck seemed to have completely abandoned the Americans. September had brought nothing but bitter disappointment. The GIs were bogged down by the weather. They lived in rain, mud, and discomfort. Most of the time they were wet and hungry. Some days the rations were late reaching the lines. Some days they never came.

Vicious little battles were fought daily. Men died for a few yards of muddy earth. The pattern of the warfare did not change. The Americans hung on to the roadblocks and ridges southeast of Aachen, and the Germans tried to push them out.

The capture of Stolberg was highly important for the

Yanks. It marked their deepest penetration of the Siegfried line and also gave U. S. troops a jumping-off place from which to launch a complete breakthrough, for beyond Stolberg the Cologne plain stretched all the way to the Rhine River. However, no further eastward movement could be made with Aachen still in German hands. The enemy garrison in that city had to be eliminated.

Accordingly, on Monday, September 25, the First Army CO issued an order to all units under his command:

"Effective immediately . . . a well coordinated attack aimed at taking the city of Aachen . . . will be launched. . . . Once Aachen is secured . . . we shall drive eastward, capture Düren and Cologne, and reach the western bank of the Rhine River by 1 October. . . ."

If General Hodges actually believed that his army could capture Aachen and reach the Rhine River in seven days, he was overly optimistic. The GIs at the front shrugged when they heard the order. One outspoken GI declared, "What the General wants and what he'll get are two different things. We can't take Aachen and reach the Rhine in a week—unless the Germans decide to quit cold, which isn't very likely!"

The First Army's basic plan for capturing Aachen remained unchanged. The 30th Division was to push south, the 1st Division hammer its way north, thus encircling the city. As this maneuver was being accomplished, White and Blue Battalions, 26th Infantry, would storm Aachen itself.

The task confronting the Americans that last week in

September was far greater than it had been only a fortnight earlier. Instead of weakening, the Germans in Aachen had gained strength. A fine highway led to Aachen from Cologne and Düren. Every night, truckloads of food, munitions, and reinforcements rolled in from the east, unhampered by U. S. planes still grounded by the miserable weather.

To implement Hodges' order, the Americans had to capture the high ground that dominated the Aachen-Cologne-Düren road. They had to take many heavily defended hills and ridges to accomplish this. The key point in that hilly and rocky terrain was Crucifix Hill, a steep, 800-yard-long ridge which rose near the town of Verlautenheide, two and one-half miles east of Aachen. Crucifix Hill took its name from a huge wooden cross which stood on its crest. That religious symbol was put to a use for which it had never been intended. The Germans set up an artillery observation post inside the hollow cross.

The mission to take Crucifix Hill and the other ridges was assigned to the 16th Infantry and the 18th Infantry Regiments. Those units fanned out toward Verlautenheide at dawn, September 25.

The infantrymen sloshed in the mud behind their tanks through German minefields. They were cut down by the hidden machine guns and deadly artillery of the Siegfried line. Verlautenheide must have seemed impregnable to the tired GIs who battered against its defenses. The American advance moved at a torturous pace, and a life was lost for every foot of ground gained.

The rain had made a wallow of every road and

meadow. Tanks were trapped in rain-soaked marshes. One 18th Infantry company sloshed past some medium tanks which were supposed to be leading the GI attack on a fortified village. Instead, the armored vehicles were drawn up at the roadside.

"How come you're not going ahead?" a rifleman called to a tanker sitting atop his vehicle.

"It's too muddy," the tankman said.

"How about that!" the foot soldier cried indignantly. "Too muddy for tanks—but not for us!'

"Buddy, get wise! We're expendable—but tanks cost dough!" another infantryman said.

Soon the fighting around Verlautenheide became stalemated. The attack which General Hodges had hoped would be able to reach the Rhine River by October 1 slopped to a halt, mired down in the sodden earth.

Casualties rose on both sides. Snipers picked off unwary men. U. S. tanks skidded across muddy flats to lead vain infantry attacks on German strongpoints. Artillery duels went on for hours at a time. There was seldom any relief from German 88's and American 105's as shrapnel whistled overhead.

German armor appeared in growing numbers, and the Yanks had to beat off Nazi armored assaults. Tanks fought tanks in inconclusive clashes. Nothing significant was achieved; neither army had the strength to break the other. The Americans could wrench only a few yards of ground from the Germans in the all-day fighting. But foot by foot, the enemy was being pushed back, and the GIs inched up the ridge.

American progress was so slow that it scarcely showed on the situation maps in regimental CP's and division headquarters. At the front, the GIs in mud ate cold C rations and cursed the war, the rain, and the Germans, in that order. They dug in on the rain-drenched slopes of Crucifix Hill and the other heights for which they were fighting.

Every night, patrols crept out into no man's land. Men were killed or mangled by mines. The Germans had sown the hillsides with a particularly nasty land mine known as Bouncing Betty: When stepped on, a powerful spring hurled the device into the air and it exploded at about the height of a man's belt line.

When they retreated from a position, the enemy rigged ingenious booby traps which killed and maimed many Americans. In one cottage, the water taps were wired to an explosive charge. A hapless GI turned a faucet and was blown to bits. The battle was an endless, grinding misery. A man needed stubborn and unyielding courage to survive. . . .

The U. S. 16th and 18th Infantry Regiments bore the brunt of this murderous warfare. At times, Nazi resistance bordered on madness. When pillboxes ran out of ammunition, the enemy fought with trench knives and clubbed rifles. The Germans made suicide attacks, charging straight into American machine guns. The frenzied defense was carried out by the SS units to which the enemy high command had entrusted the ridges. Apparently, Field Marshal Model did not have confidence in the Wehrmacht for such a vital assignment.

"I never before had seen men such as those Nazis at Verlautenheide," Colonel Frederick W. Gibb, 16th Infantry CO, later wrote. "You had to kill one to stop him!"

Tech Sergeant James W. (Jake) Lindsay, Charlie (C) Company, 16th Infantry, a holder of the Congressional Medal of Honor, remarked, "Either those Krauts were crazy or else they were the bravest soldiers in the world. They'd run cheering into our line of fire as if we were spraying them with a garden hose instead of bullets. When a man was hit, he'd crawl on his hands and knees, but he kept coming."

It seemed impossible that the Germans could maintain such frenzied resistance. But at Verlautenheide they showed no signs of weakening. They took enormous losses. A duty roster captured on September 27 in the CP of a crack SS battalion showed that only forty out of an original five hundred men were available for duty. Yet the Americans could make no headway.

U. S. morale sagged. The war which seemed to have been won in August still roared on in late September. Less than two weeks earlier the Germans had appeared beaten. Now they fought harder than ever. General Hodges' order to reach the Rhine River by October 1 became a bitter joke among GIs.

White and Blue Battalions, 26th Infantry, assigned the capture of Aachen, did no better than the men striving to take the ridges near the city. The Germans had made a fortress of every house and cellar in Aachen's environs.

Colonel J. F. R. Seitz, 26th Infantry CO, declared, "The worst fighting of the war is still before us. It's going to be tough, but by God, we'll break the Germans!"

With the battle for Aachen at a veritable standstill, the soaring optimism of the summer turned to sullen determination. In the United States, the American people rolled up their sleeves and went to work harder than ever. "Okay, the Germans are rough. But we'll show 'em we're rougher!" the Americans muttered.

A few bright beacons pierced the gloom of war. The lights had gone on in London for the first time in five years to end the long blackout as the danger of German air raids finally faded. In the Channel ports of Deal, Folkestone, and Dover, people danced in the streets when the German long-range cannon that had been shelling the towns from Cape Gris Nez, France, since June, 1940, were captured and blown up by British troops.

Best of all, no more robot bombs fell on London. During the last week of September, British forces took the launching sites in Belgium and Holland. Far away, in the Pacific, General MacArthur's island-hopping troops were drawing closer and closer to the Philippines and the general was soon to make good his promise, "I shall return!"

On the western front, at Aachen, the war situation was still grim and undecided. But nothing could stifle the caustic wit of the American GIs. The two battalions of the 26th Infantry Regiment fighting in the city's suburbs promptly dubbed their objective "Achin' Aachen." That name caught on and in GI parlance any unpleasant job was known as an "Achin' Aachen."

The war went on in an endless passage of miserable

days. Then, on Sunday, October 1, the day the Americans should have reached the western shore of the Rhine River, an abrupt change took place. A blaze of sunshine heralded daybreak. Instead of a biting wind, gentle breezes riffled the ruined crops in the shell-torn German fields. Mutilated tree branches swayed in soft gusts. The sky was cobalt blue with no trace of the somber clouds that had darkened it for so long.

The fighting petered out in the sunlight; the battle din gradually lessened until the report of a single rifle raised echoes across a still valley. The artillery guns were silent as if in some wondrous manner the war had ended and all was peaceful again. Perhaps the unofficial truce had come because nobody in either army wanted to die on such a morning.

Men poked cautiously out of their foxholes, blinking in the unaccustomed brightness. Mud-stained soldiers stripped themselves to the waist and basked in the sun. Groups of Americans and Germans stood up within sight of one another, but no one raised a weapon. Birds chirped merrily among the truncated trees in a copse near Verlautenheide, only a mile from shell-pocked Crucifix Hill.

The respite from war was brief. At 0800 (8:00 A.M.) a loud, droning noise was heard in the distance behind the American lines. The GIs, taking advantage of the lull, looked up from cleaning rifles, writing letters, or snoozing as the sound grew louder and more definable.

"It's the fly-boys!" someone cried gleefully.

Sure enough, high above, trailing fluffy vapor streams, came scores of planes in V-shaped formations. Heavy bombers, medium bombers, and fighters passed over the lines as though in review. The American infantrymen leaped up and cheered as the huge air armada droned past their positions toward the Germans.

The enemy's antiaircraft (AA) guns thudded frantically. Dirty gray smoke puffs marked bursting flak, and the sky became dotted with exploding AA shells; but the planes flew on without hesitation.

Fighters and fighter-bombers peeled off to strafe and blast the front-line Germans. Heavy and medium bombers moved in stately procession deep into the German heartland. Before that Sunday was over, they dropped 4,000–5,000 tons of bombs on Cologne (population 700,000) and Duisburg (population 410,000).

The American fighters and fighter-bombers concentrated on the Germans around Verlautenheide with special attention to those entrenched atop Crucifix Hill.

"I watched through my glasses as the Hill disappeared in the smoke of bursting bombs. Thunderbolts and Mustangs whipped back and forth strafing the Germans," an 18th Infantry officer recalled. "Now and then, a big explosion went off and flames shot a hundred feet in the air. I figured our boys had hit enemy ammunition dumps. Not a single Luftwaffe plane showed. Our flyboys ruled the sky. All around me GIs were jumping up and down, yelling as though it was a football game. I yelled too, but inside I felt like crying. The poor Krauts, I thought, even they don't deserve to die on such a day."

At the same time that the big air attack hit Verlautenheide, the 30th Infantry Division unleashed a massive attack of its own about ten miles north of Aachen. A hundred heavy field guns poured a fearful barrage across the Wurm River from the vicinity of Heerlen, Holland, on the German border, to start the U. S. offensive. As shells blasted the Germans on the eastern side of the river, the 119th Infantry Regiment moved forward behind a group of Sherman tanks.

Companies of infantry, bayonets glinting in the sunlight, slid down the five-foot-high western bank of the river and struggled through the icy, waist-deep water of the turbid twelve-foot-wide river which served at that point as the boundary separating Belgium, Holland, and Germany.

Up the steep slope on the German side of the stream scrambled the GIs. They found enemy soldiers, dazed by the furious barrage, staggering about, eager to surrender. Submachine-gun slinging MP's hustled the shocked prisoners across the river where waiting trucks hauled them to compounds.

Flame-throwing tanks swiftly snuffed out the desultory resistance that flickered from a row of German pillboxes. For the most part, the 119th Infantry GIs pushed into Germany without meeting serious opposition. By noon, the regiment had broken through to an area where fantastically shaped slag heaps rose to heights of thirty to forty feet to give the terrain a weird appearance.

After hard fighting to take these piles which the enemy used as machine-gun nests, the 119th swung northeast toward Ubach, a strategic link of the Siegfried line.

The other 30th Division infantry regiments, the 117th

and 120th, plus 2nd and 7th Armored Division tanks, drove ahead on a nine-mile-wide front in the direction of three more Siegfried line strongpoints—Geilenkirchen, Beggendorf, and Merkstein. These towns had to be captured before the 30th Infantry Division could safely swing south and link up with the 1st Division to snap closed the cordon around Aachen.

The drive was aided by other XIX Corps troops. The 29th Division opened a big attack on the Siegfried line still farther to the north while the 2nd and 7th Armored Divisions threw in every available tank to hammer the Germans in an overwhelming armored assault.

The Americans had launched the long-awaited big push.

9. THE BATTERING RAM

UBACH, GERMANY
Monday, October 2, 1944—
Wednesday, October 4, 1944

THE NOOSE TIGHTENS

CHAPTER 9

O<small>N MONDAY, OCTOBER</small> 2, the day after the American attack had jumped off, General Dwight Eisenhower broadcast a message to the 8,000,000 slave laborers in Germany. The Allied Supreme Commander said:

"I am speaking to all of you who have been forced to work against your will for the enemy within his borders. Begin now to leave the factories! The hour for action has come! Organized cells of foreign workers inside the Reich will take immediate action according to prearranged plans. Act wisely! Do not underestimate the Gestapo! Do not be provoked into unorganized actions. . . ."

Nothing the Americans had done before aroused so much fear among Germans as did Eisenhower's summons to the enslaved workers. For five years the Nazi masters had forced their captives to toil in war plants at the hardest physical labor without payment or proper food. When a slave could no longer keep up the pace the Nazis demanded, he was shipped to a death camp and the gas chamber.

Now these gray-faced slaves had been incited to revolt, and the Germans trembled at the shocking thought of angry slave millions rising up to take a terrible revenge. Factory foremen were issued side arms, and special guards patrolled the workshops. The Nazis even sought to head off an insurrection by issuing the slaves good food and decent clothing. This sudden change in the treatment of the workers was an immediate result of Eisenhower's broadcast.

The general's call to action had other effects as well. A spate of machinery breakdowns slowed production in German munitions plants. Critical parts were damaged and tools mysteriously broken. Complaints came to Berlin from the front that many artillery shells proved to be duds when fired. All over Germany, factory buildings and equipment were destroyed or damaged by a rash of fires.

The slaves were obeying General Eisenhower. The faceless, anonymous people whom the German scorned as inferior beings fought bravely in this secret warfare. There were no spectacular riots, no widespread mutinies, no turbulent outbreaks. The silent war of sabotage bit deeply into the German war effort, and though the Gestapo seized and executed hundreds of foreign workers, the sabotage went on without interruption.

At last, even the Gestapo called a halt to the executions because the Germans needed slaves to man the factories and to produce material for the front. So the Nazis had to endure the sabotage while the Gestapo vainly strove to find the leaders of the movement.

The slaves grew more daring every day. Allied agents smuggled weapons and tiny incendiary devices to them. The underground activists made the Germans so jittery that the Nazis even believed a rumor of a poison plot by the slave workers. It was whispered that slave kitchen help in a number of Nazi headquarters had somehow obtained vials of a deadly new poison which took effect in forty-eight hours and was impossible to detect, being tasteless and odorless. For a while, many Gestapo, SS, and Nazi party mess halls were almost deserted at meal times, but the slaves working there gained weight on the excellent food their masters dared not touch.

While slave resistance was limited mainly to sabotage, a few mass demonstrations also took place. The biggest were at Eisenach and Dessau, where French, Belgian, and Dutch workers seized a barracks and defied the Nazis by singing their national anthems. The Nazis took no punitive measures against the demonstrators because they were fearful of touching off a chain reaction of similar disturbances. But when the workers actually went on strike, the Nazis acted. SS troops were rushed in and many executions followed.

Meanwhile, on the Aachen front, the fighting blazed without letup. Interest was centered on Ubach, a coal-mining town situated two miles inside Germany from the eastern bank of the Wurm River where it ran along the Dutch border and five miles due north of Aachen. Ubach had strategic importance, and its capture was vital to the 30th Division's attack. The town blocked the division's progress toward its prime objective, the link-up with the 1st Division. The Germans knew this, and at Ubach the Siegfried line was especially well manned and strongly fortified. The Americans prepared themselves for a major effort to smash through.

"Ubach has to be taken. The outcome of the whole Aachen operation depends on what you do here," Major General Leland Hobbs, CO of the 30th Division, told the men of the 119th Infantry Regiment who were to storm the town.

At dawn, October 2, the GIs hurled themselves against the German fortifications. The attack was preceded by a tremendous artillery barrage. More than 2,000 shells were fired on the German positions.

"We used every round we had," an artillery officer said. "If the truckers hadn't brought up more ammunition that afternoon we couldn't have fired another shot."

The onslaught was to have been supported by an air strike as well, but after Sunday's beautiful weather, the skies clouded over, the rain and the fog returned, and the Army Air Corps planes were grounded once again.

Fighting raged all day Monday, October 2, and early on Tuesday, a 30th Division spokesman gleefully announced, "We have broken through most of the Siegfried line around Ubach."

Despite these early successes, the battle for Ubach was far from over. The 119th Infantry still had a lot of hard fighting to do. After slugging through the Siegfried line fortifications, they found the Germans entrenched in the coal mines that ringed Ubach. Hundreds of feet underground, GIs hunted the foe in mine tunnels, passageways, and corridors. Clearing out the enemy was difficult. Small groups ambushed each other. Often the struggle was waged at close quarters.

The Americans fortunately made a lucky find to end that phase of the fighting. An infantry squad took a mine superintendent's office and discovered there a master map which showed the location of every tunnel in the coal mine. Demolition teams were then able to plant TNT charges which sealed off the hidden Germans beneath tons of dirt, stone, shale, and rubble.

But after the enemy in the coal mines had been eliminated, the 119th had to fight from street to street, house to house, and room to room in Ubach. Even with some troops actually inside the town, a great obstacle still faced the regiment. The Germans had fortified Schloss Rimberg, which dominated the town from the hillside where it had been standing for eight centuries.

Atop its barren hillside, Schloss Rimberg resembled a story-book castle with its moat, drawbridge, keep, buttresses, and battlements. Despite its great age and medieval appearance, the Schloss had been converted into an excellent twentieth-century bastion. Machine guns poked from firing slits that had been meant for crossbows. Soldiers with automatic rifles guarded ramparts where men in chain mail had once fought off an enemy.

The Germans in the castle had to be eliminated before Ubach could be taken. Red Battalion, 119th Infantry, supported by two batteries of 105-mm howitzers and a section of Long Toms, was given this dangerous and difficult job. At 0400 (4:00 A.M.) Wednesday, October 4, the guns let loose on Schloss Rimberg in a freezing rainstorm. A huge 204-mm howitzer that the GIs had dubbed "Li'l Abner" made such a loud noise that a jeep driver who had never before heard the gun skidded off the road as the howitzer let loose while he was riding by. Soldiers hauled his jeep out of the mud and the shaken driver gasped, "That danged gun almost scared me to death. Why the blast nearly blew me out of my shoes."

"Just hope it's doing the same to the Krauts up there in that fancy stone pile," a GI remarked, pointing at Schloss Rimberg.

The artillery bombardment of the castle went on for two hours. By 0600 (6:00 A.M.), the Schloss was hidden in smoke, but its SS garrison gave no sign of surrendering. At 0700 (7:00 A.M.) Red Battalion, 119th Infantry, rushed the venerable stronghold. The men scaled the moat under furious automatic arms fire from the Germans; but the enemy could not halt the GIs who swarmed over the walls and forced an entry into the castle. Wild fighting raged in every part of the Schloss, from its tower to its dark dungeon. GIs and Germans fought with grenades, knives, bayonets, and rifle butts. Chambers that had once echoed to clanking armor now reverberated with grenade explosions. The deadly hand-to-hand struggle raged up and down the stone stairways for five hours.

At the end, only a single squad of SS men still held out in a tower room. They were trapped up there with no chance to escape except by leaping to the ground many feet below. However, the SS men finally rejected this alternative and gave up to the Americans.

The grimy victors explored the castle they had captured. Peering into a grenade-splattered banquet hall, one Yank grinned broadly. "What a scrap that was—right out of a Grade B Hollywood movie," he laughed.

"Sure, buddy. Only this was for real," a comrade said.

As Schloss Rimberg was falling to the Americans, the U. S. 117th and 120th Infantry Regiments captured a stretch of high ground which enabled the 30th Division artillery to shell the München-Gladbach–Aachen road, the westernmost of the two main arteries by which Aachen was supplied. At about the same time, XIX Corps artillery came within range of Beggendorf and started shelling that Siegfried line redoubt.

Ten miles south of all this combat, White and Blue Battalions, 16th Infantry, 1st Division, were trying to consolidate newly won positions on the heights near Verlautenheide. Without warning, at 2335 (11:35 P.M.), October 3, the 27th Wehrmacht Division hurled a crushing attack against Blue Battalion, 16th Infantry, in the sector held by King (K) Company.

The first hint King Company had of the German action came when enemy 88-mm guns began to shell the position with increasing fury. In less than an hour, the enemy poured 3,500 shells on the company's lines. At 2430 (12:30 A.M.) waves of German infantry rushed the shell-dazed Yanks. This attack was supported by a dozen medium tanks, eight large self-propelled guns (SPG's) and a novel German weapon—a self-propelled dynamite charge known as "Goliath" which was to be exploded in the midst of the American position.

Although shaken by the foe's artillery barrage, the Yanks rallied to meet the enemy. Almost incredibly, King Company had taken few casualties during the bombardment. The GIs had learned to dig their foxholes deep.

The advancing Germans came on briskly behind the tanks and SPG's which lobbed shells on the embattled Americans. But after the pounding they had taken, the GIs ignored this fire. As the enemy reached the base of the ridge line, the Americans sent up flares which briefly illuminated the ground over which the Germans were advancing. The GIs on the ridge clearly saw the approaching enemy troops in the flare-light.

German tanks lurched from the direction of Verlautenheide to lead the infantry in line with the SPG's and the ponderous Goliath. U. S. artillery liaison officers had only a few moments before the flares burned out to pick targets, estimate range, and pass on fire orders to their batteries. In seconds, the observers were phoning back to the gun positions. Soon, American shells were landing on the Germans. A direct hit quickly destroyed the Goliath and caused numerous casualties among the enemy. Accurate American marksmanship soon knocked out four SPG's, but the German medium tanks waddled untouched through the avalanche of Yank shells. A hurry call went out to Task Force Hogan for armored assistance in repelling the Germans. Colonel Hogan's Shermans sped into the battle and met the panzers in a slugging match that left the enemy vehicles completely wrecked, twisted heaps of smoldering metal.

Once their armor had been smashed, the German infantrymen faltered and the Wehrmacht division lost the initiative. Still the Germans continued the assault for three hours longer, vainly searching for a soft spot in the U. S. defense.

Apparently the enemy was unable to comprehend that the barrage which preceded the attack had not broken American morale. The Germans had counted heavily on their artillery and refused to concede that it failed in its purpose. Although the German barrage had been severe, the Yanks on the line met the foe with withering small arms and mortars until the Wehrmacht had to admit defeat and retreated back into Verlautenheide.

Throughout the first week in October, the tempo of the fighting north and south of Aachen seldom slackened. Rain fell every day, all day long, and the steady downpour piled misery upon hardship. Wounded or injured GIs suffered terribly; front-line aid stations were always kept busy, and rows of stretchers upon which maimed and torn men lay moaning were left for hours in the open without shelter from the wind and the rain. Ambulances made dozens of trips to haul casualties from the front. Doctors and nurses worked around the clock tending the wounded but could not cope with the avalanche of pain and agony that swamped them.

"Casualty clearing stations looked like pictures I had seen of the Civil War. Suffering men called for help, but no one could treat them. They had to wait their turn, sometimes a whole day. It was about the most awful thing I ever saw," a medical detachment orderly remembered.

Despite German resistance, bad weather, and every other difficulty, the American pincers slowly began to close in on Aachen. The greatest U. S. pressure was applied five to six miles north of the beleaguered city where the 30th Division entered Beggendorf on Friday, October 6, after a sharp fight. The Germans had ten big Tiger tanks to defend the town, but Long Tom shells exploded the enemy fuel storage tanks there and the Germans had no gasoline for the Tigers. Unable to move his panzers, the foe dug them in and used the vehicles with great effect as pillboxes, until American demolition specialists did their work.

As U. S. Infantry seized Beggendorf, 2nd Armored Division tanks rolled into Geilenkirchen closely followed by Blue Battalion, 117th Infantry. The foot soldiers met such strong resistance that a GI averred, "I've been in every battle since Normandy, but we never ran into anything like this since Saint-Lô—and I'd have bet my last buck that nothing could ever equal that scrap. . . ."

Near Herbach, a few miles north of Aachen, the Americans penetrated a deep woods, and of the fighting in that sector a *New York Times* war correspondent wrote:

"This forest fighting is like a bad dream. Our men move among pine trees in eerie, shadowy silence which is suddenly broken by gunfire. . . . You cannot see more than twenty-five yards in any direction. Wounded men fall in the thick underbrush and die there unseen and unattended. . . . This is ground war at its starkest. . . ."

The first weekend in October, Saturday and Sunday, October 7 and 8, brought startling changes in the military situation, for in that period the Germans suddenly collapsed north of Aachen, and every major enemy resistance center was overrun by jubilant Yanks.

On Saturday, October 7, the sun made one of its rare appearances. It was a fleeting one, but lasted long enough for the Army Air Corps to send up hundreds of planes which raked the German lines with bombs, bullets, and rockets. Truck convoys heading into Aachen along the Cologne-Düren-Aachen road were blasted. The planes roved up and down the Aachen sector smashing every target in sight.

The next day, October 8, the Germans caved in and the 30th Division took Alsdorf, Eschweiler, and Merkstein in rapid succession to open a salient through the Siegfried line ten miles deep and nine miles wide. By nightfall of that crucial Sunday the 117th, 119th, and 120th Infantry Regiments counted a haul of more than 2,000 prisoners, and 119th Infantry patrols probed southward to make contact with the 1st Division.

In that unit's sector Red Battalion, 18th Infantry, finally captured Verlautenheide after repulsing a Nazi counterattack which lasted from 0400, Monday, October 9, until noon. Once the Germans had been beaten off, Red Battalion moved on. By 1730 (5:30 P.M.), it had possession of Verlautenheide, Crucifix Hill, and all the important ridges for which so much blood had been shed.

From the crests of these heights, 18th Infantry GIs could see Aachen's red tile roof tops and the spires of the cathedral a scant two miles away. Enthusiasm rose among the Americans when the news spread that all roads into Aachen were being shelled.

"We've got 'em now!" a soldier exulted.

He was not quite right. Although in bad straits, the Germans were not yet whipped. They still had strength and fighting spirit. This was particularly true in the SS battalions. An indication of how dangerous the enemy could be was brought home to the American troops after they captured Alsdorf. In that sector, an SS colonel called for volunteers to make a counterattack on the town, which was of great strategic value to the Germans. Alsdorf sat astride the Linnich-Aachen highway, an excellent secondary road by which the city could be supplied. The SS officer's aim was to retake Alsdorf and keep the road open.

Every man who volunteered took a blood oath that he would fight until death. After that mass ceremony, the four hundred German volunteers attacked Alsdorf aided by four Mark VI Tiger tanks.

The four tanks broke into the town, but the SS colonel and most of his men were cut down by American automatic weapons and mortars as they sought to follow the

Tigers. The U. S. 117th Infantry, which held Alsdorf, sent out its bazooka gunners in a deadly game of hide-and-seek with the four panzers. Three German tanks were quickly put out of commission, but the fourth got away unscathed. Soon, every GI in Alsdorf had joined the panzer hunt. Up and down the cobbled streets the chase led, but the tank somehow managed to elude all the pursuers.

The GI's dubbed the tank the *Phantom Kraut,* for it appeared and disappeared with startling ease, evading every trap the Americans set. The closest the Yanks came to the *Phantom Kraut* was when an Able (A) Company lieutenant spotted the vehicle in a side street and saw two crewmen cautiously peering from the raised hatch to get their bearings. The American officer killed both Germans with his carbine, but before any damage could be done to the tank the hatch cover clanged shut and the *Phantom Kraut* lurched away to be seen no more in Alsdorf.

By Monday, October 9, the U. S. First Army was less than three miles from snapping shut the ring around Aachen, for only that distance separated the 30th Division and the 1st Division. In rear areas everyone behaved as if the city had been captured and the battle won.

However, a front-line officer, Lieutenant Colonel John Williamson (CO, Blue Battalion, 18th Infantry), sounded a sober note: "The enemy is not yet beaten, nor do we hold Aachen. Much blood is still to be shed, both theirs and ours . . . before the final victory. . . ."

The situation at Aachen troubled General Hodges. His

men were still stalled in the city's suburbs where they had been fighting since September 25. His hopes of reaching the Rhine by October 1 had been dashed. No one dared remind the general about that rash and unrealistic order.

Hodges was determined to end the battle of Aachen. He decided on certain drastic steps to accomplish this, but before putting them into effect the First Army's CO called a conference to be held at noon, Monday, October 9, in his headquarters south of Aachen. He invited to the meeting the commanding officers of the 30th Division and the 1st Division with their regimental commanders. The fate of the American offensive at Aachen rested on the outcome of that gathering.

10. ULTIMATUM

AACHEN, GERMANY
Tuesday, October 10, 1944

AACHEN, GATEWAY INTO GERMANY

CHAPTER 10

THE ACTION WHICH General Hodges proposed to his council of war was this: On Tuesday, October 10, an ultimatum would be sent under a flag of truce to Colonel Gerhardt Wilck, who commanded the Aachen garrison. As written by Hodges, the ultimatum said in part:

> TO THE GERMAN COMMANDING OFFICER: Aachen is now completely surrounded by American forces. . . . We shall take the city either by receiving its immediate and unconditional surrender or by attacking and destroying it. . . . The choice is yours. . . . Our

assault will begin 24 hours after you receive this message. . . . You have a grave responsibility. . . . The lives of many civilians are in your hands. . . . And Aachen is not alone. . . . Its fate may become that of all German cities. . . .

Lt. Gen. Courtney H. Hodges
Commanding U. S. First Army

An officer who attended the meeting later wrote: "We all felt it was high time for such a step. The General had been reluctant to threaten Aachen with annihilation because we knew many civilians were still in the city. Besides, it was the first big German city in our path. All of us had hoped the Nazis wouldn't fight for it as they did. We figured they'd retreat across the Rhine and try to hold us there. But after a month of fierce resistance, General Hodges finally decided that either the Germans must surrender at once, or we'd level Aachen. Every officer present agreed with this course and enthusiastically supported the General."

For humane reasons, General Hodges felt the civilians and noncombatants in Aachen should be forewarned of the holocaust they might have to face. Intelligence officers estimated that almost 15,000 civilians had remained in the city and the First Army CO believed it possible to cause a rift between these German civilians and the military.

On Hodges' orders the First Army Psychological Warfare Detachment prepared a leaflet aimed at achieving that purpose.

The circular read:

> PEOPLE OF AACHEN!
> Act quickly! Go to those responsible. Make them stop this useless bloodshed and destruction. The time has come for you and your civil leaders to speak boldly. Tomorrow may be too late! On our airfields, bombers are awaiting final orders to take off. Our artillery surrounding your city is waiting to fire. Our troops are ready for the final attack. . . . You must decide what will happen. . . . The alternative is immediate surrender or total destruction. . . .

General Hodges received sanction from the highest quarters for his "surrender or die" ultimatum. General Dwight Eisenhower officially approved. Even more important, a spokesman for President Roosevelt, the Secretary of War, Henry L. Stimson, declared:

"No German cities may expect immunity from destruction so long as they are maintained as part of the enemy's battle line. . . . German civilians will have to bear the burden of any decision imposed on them by their military leaders. . . ."

According to Intelligence reports, the time was right for the ultimatum. Although the Aachen garrison was still fighting hard, internal trouble and dissension was rampant in the city. SS troops had so incensed the Wehrmacht that clashes had taken place between the two branches.

This was learned on Sunday, October 8, when a 26th Infantry patrol had captured some Wehrmacht men. The Germans told their captors how the SS treated other troops. The prisoners expressed great bitterness over SS oppression. That very day, nineteen Wehrmacht officers and enlisted men had been executed by an SS firing squad in an Aachen public square because they had protested against Elite Corps arrogance and brutality. The SS had labeled the dead men traitors and warned that the same fate lay in store for all Wehrmacht personnel displaying hostility toward the SS.

"Those drunken SS beasts run the city," a Wehrmacht prisoner cried. "It's more than a man can bear to see them looting homes, beating up civilians, and turning their guns on us! I tell you they are madmen! You will never make them surrender. You will be fighting mad dogs, not German soldiers!"

"Don't worry, Fritzie," a GI said. "We'll muzzle 'em. So don't let it throw you."

Tuesday, October 10, the day after General Hodges had met with his officers, arrangements were completed for delivering the ultimatum to the Germans. At 0900 (9:00 A.M.) three U. S. soldiers (two lieutenants and one private, first class) emerged from a partially demolished schoolhouse in Brand, an Aachen suburb, about a mile from the city's center. The wrecked school was being used as a CP by White Battalion, 26th Infantry.

The men were First Lieutenant George Laffley, who

bore Hodges' note in a Manila portfolio; German-speaking First Lieutenant William Boehme, the group's interpreter; and Pfc Kenneth Kading, who carried a five-foot-square flag made of white pillowcases and nailed to a short staff.

The trio paraded down the long hill that led from Brand to Aachen. Each man had on a clean, freshly pressed uniform. (The pressing job had been done in a Brand tailor shop that White Battalion had captured intact with the tailor and all his equipment.) The truce party's combat boots were polished to a gloss and the men wore white parade gloves.

The group marched to the very edges of Aachen where piles of rubble marked German lines. To the east, only a few leaden clouds hung in the sky amid wide patches of blue. A cool wind caught the white truce flag and it snapped briskly over Kading's head. For a change, there was no hint of rain.

As Laffley, Boehme, and Kading strode past, unshaven GIs in foxholes cheered and shouted encouragement to them. A thousand pairs of binoculars followed their progress from the American side—and the German, as well. Generals Hodges, Huebner, and Collins stood with Colonel J. F. R. Seitz (CO, 26th Infantry) and Lieutenant Colonel Derrill M. Daniel (CO, White Battalion), glasses focused on the three stalwart figures until they were lost in the debris of the Nazi positions.

A German officer stepped from a shell-torn house and raised his hand to halt the American truce party. "What do you want?" he asked in English.

"I have a message from our commander to yours," Laffley said.

"What is the nature of the message?"

"My orders are to deal only with your commander," Laffley stated firmly.

"Very well. I will take you to him," the German agreed.

In accordance with accepted military procedure, the Americans were blindfolded so they could not see enemy troop dispositions. They were then led to a staff car. After a brief drive, the vehicle stopped before a four-story stone building in the heart of Aachen.

Colonel Gerhardt Wilck, his lean frame draped in a natty uniform, a monocle tightly clamped in his right eye, waited in the doorway. At his side was an aide, a captain, with cheeks crisscrossed by Heidelberg dueling scars.

Laffley and Boehme, still blindfolded, were assisted from the car, while Kading remained in the rear seat holding the truce flag high.

Colonel Wilck wasted no time. "State your business," he snapped in German.

After Lieutenant Boehme explained why the truce team had come, Laffley held out the portfolio containing the ultimatum and Wilck's aide snatched it brusquely from his hand.

"Colonel, I have the American communication," the aide told Wilck.

"Good. Then these men have finished their business with us. Give them safe passage to their own lines," Wilck ordered.

Laffley and Boehme saluted. The Germans responded and the American officers were escorted to the car again and transported through the German defenses. The blindfolds were removed at the place where they had entered the German lines. The officer who first met them said, "Enough blood has been spilled. I hope your terms are accepted. Now, *auf Wiedersehen*. We shall meet again. Perhaps on earth. Perhaps in heaven. Who knows?"

He snapped to stiff attention and saluted. Boehme and Laffley returned the soldierly gesture and then fell in to flank Kading. Up the long hill they marched in cadence, conscious of the German eyes trained on them.

At 1055 (10:55 A.M.), Laffley, Boehme, and Kading reached White Battalion CP and reported to General Hodges.

The First Army Commander glanced at his watch. "If there is no prior communication from the enemy, we shall open our attack at this hour tomorrow."

The only fighting in Aachen on October 10 broke out in the northeastern sector of the city where desperate Germans tried to hack through the American cordon, but tanks and artillery fire snuffed out this attempt.

At 1400 (2:00 P.M.), 1st Division artillery on Crucifix Hill opened a thirty-minute-long bombardment; but the shells that exploded in Aachen contained leaflets urging surrender, and the sheets fluttered down on Aachen like a paper blizzard.

In one 5th Field Artillery battery, a gun crewman rammed a leaflet-packed shell into his gun. "I hope the Krauts're in a reading mood." He laughed.

119

"Maybe we're wasting our time," another artilleryman said. "Maybe they won't get the message."

"So we'll switch back to HE and blast 'em, instead of tossing bed-time stories," the first soldier said. "You have to handle a German like you would a balky mule. If he won't listen to reason you pick up a club and pound sense into him."

If the personnel of the First Army Psychological Warfare Detachment had expected their leaflet to bring on a mass exodus from Aachen, they were disappointed. Only a handful of civilians and a few bedraggled soldiers entered the American lines after the propaganda barrage.

At first light on Wednesday, October 11, 26th Infantry outposts reported bedsheets and pillowcases hanging from windows in houses near the front. This did not indicate a general capitulation by the enemy. They had been placed by civilians, and squads of SS soon removed them.

The morning hours ticked away. In the White Battalion CP, at 1050 (10:50 A.M.), a mere five minutes before the ultimatum was to expire, General Hodges announced, "I shall grant the Germans an hour's grace. If no word is received from them by then, we will attack according to plan."

It was a sparkling day, perfect flying weather. As the deadline neared, tension mounted in the CP and among the expectant American troops. Everyone with binoculars scanned the German lines for signs of surrender flags. Nothing stirred in Aachen. The red tile roofs were slashes of brilliant color in the sunlight; the cathedral's spires jutted gracefully like tall sentries guarding the brooding city.

Within the CP, the officers closely watched General Hodges as time ran out. Precisely at 1155 (11:55 A.M.) the First Army CO rose from his camp chair. "Gentlemen, we've waited long enough. Let's get to work," he said quietly.

The 1st Division Artillery Chief, Brigadier General Clift Andrus, picked up the handset of a field telephone. "All batteries open fire immediately," he ordered.

Concurrently, the take-off signal was flashed to forward operational airstrips crowded with Lightning (P-38), Mustang (P-47), and Thunderbolt (P-51) fighter-bombers and Marauder (B-26) medium bombers.

The moment of truth had come for Aachen.

Not even the most combat-hardened GI had ever experienced an artillery bombardment of the intensity that followed General Andrus's order. From noon until 1500 (3:00 P.M.) two hundred field guns pounded Aachen with a total of 16,500 HE shells.

Awe-stricken infantrymen sat beside their foxholes and gaped as tremendous explosions rocked the city. The guns had scarcely begun to shoot when Army Air Corps planes arrived over the target. The fighter-bombers swept in at roof-top level to strafe the Germans with cannon, rockets and .50 caliber machine guns. The Marauders dropped tons of heavy bombs and thousands of incendiaries.

Fires twinkled and danced through the gloom of

121

smoke that enshrouded Aachen. The Germans fought back with stubborn courage; flak batteries kept shooting at the U. S. planes until the guns were bombed out. But despite the massive bombings, a few AA batteries were still in action as the planes winged away.

"The Germans are trying to make another Stalingrad or Cassino of Aachen," a First Army staff officer told a group of newspapermen who had gathered at the CP to watch the destruction. "If they succeed, I'm afraid we shall have to go in there with bayonets and grenades, and that promises to be one devilish job."

At the peak of the bombardment forty-eight Wehrmacht officers and enlisted men stumbled into a 26th Infantry outpost and gave up. The Germans were so shaken by the awful shelling and bombing that some verged on hysteria.

"I've been in hell! I've been in hell!" a young German noncom screamed.

And Aachen was hell.

A haze of red brick dust rose from the shattered streets. Vast sections of the city were laid low. The two fashionable promenades Adelbertstrasse and Adelbertsteinweg were a shambles. Fallen debris and masonry were piled twenty feet high. Water spouted in noxious streams from broken sewer mains. The once luxurious Quellenhof Hotel was a ruin. Every windowpane in Aachen was broken and shards of glass dropped like crystal rain.

Amazingly, many houses still stood practically untouched. The cathedral had received only superficial damage, and the sumptuous Palace Hotel suffered nothing more than shrapnel scars on its marble façade. However, these were freakish exceptions amid the havoc. Shell holes yawned in roadways to expose a weird tangle of broken electric cables, twisted gas pipes, and blasted water mains.

The statuary in the public squares had been upended and pounded into dust. Aachen's magnificent parks were scarred and blighted. Fires raced unchecked through the wooded areas, and the air was tainted with the fumes of cordite, choking smoke, and the stench of death.

The U. S. artillery punished the city all night long, although less intensely. It was 0400 (4:00 A.M.), Thursday, October 12, when White and Blue Battalions, 26th Infantry, received orders to advance through Aachen's wreckage toward the center of the city from the east and southeast. The GIs picked their way for a number of blocks before meeting any opposition.

Then they ran into furious German resistance. The enemy emerged from the rubble like ghosts to fight in the eerie glow of a hundred fires smoldering and flaring in the carnage. The Yanks seldom had faced such desperate foes. The Germans made a stronghold of every rubble heap. It took bold American action to drive them out with grenades, bayonets, rifle butts, and flame throwers.

General J. Lawton Collins sent VII Corps 155-mm SPG's into the fray. The Long Toms fired at point-blank range against German positions. Walls toppled every time an SPG went off, and the Nazis were buried under bricks and concrete.

In the southeastern part of the city, White Battalion made good progress, riding over German defense pockets. Before October 12 ended, Lieutenant Colonel Daniel's men had captured more than five hundred prisoners; but Blue Battalion had to fight for every foot, from house to house, room to room, and "sewer to sewer," as one GI described the struggle. Few Germans were captured in this sector.

The difference was that Wehrmacht and Volkssturm units held White Battalion's area, while Blue Battalion faced SS veterans of Stalingrad.

Lieutenant John T. Corley, Blue Battalion CO, described the fighting this way: "There is no such thing as light resistance in my zone. Every position has to be stormed. . . ."

On Friday, October 13, Blue Battalion reached a huge air-raid shelter where some 3,000 Aachen civilians cowered in terror. The Yanks forced these people out and sent them to the rear at Brand. A mile-long column of Germans trudged slowly up the hill. Most of them were women, but there were many children and old men as well. Everyone carried something—a coffeepot, a vase, a pile of bedding, a bundle of clothes. Housewives trundled baby carriages piled high with household goods. A misty rain started to fall on the evacuees. As the Aacheners reached the top of the hill, some turned back, red-eyed and weeping, to look down at their city.

"This is how you treat us for fighting the Russians," a woman wailed.

Another plucked at the sleeve of an MP. "Are there any English with you?" she asked.

"No. Only Americans. Why?" the MP said.

"I hate the English. All this is their fault. Had they surrendered in nineteen hundred and forty, the war would be long over and you would not have had to destroy Aachen," the *Hausfrau* explained.

"These Krauts!" the MP said later. "They just can't seem to put the blame where it really belongs."

With each hour, Aachen became an ever more desolate wasteland. Starving cats and dogs poked in rubble for scraps of food. They sniffed at bloated corpses sprawled in streets where wide pools of stagnant water had collected. The only movement in Aachen was that of war; the only sounds the crashing of shells, the whine of bullets, the crump of grenades, and the blast of cannon. Pavement cracked and shook every time a Long Tom SPG let loose. In all that nightmare place there was no peaceful spot, no refuge, no silence.

From Berlin, Hitler broadcast to the Aachen garrison; "Fight on, Germans, my brave warriors! I am watching your magnificent battle with admiration. Fight on, fearless comrades! The armies of Russia, America, and England will yet batter themselves to pieces against German will and German iron. Sieg Heil!"

The Fuehrer's shrill voice rattled in the tinny loudspeakers that carried his words to his soldiers. But his words were lost in the darkness, the rain, and the guns; and his rantings echoed through the empty wilderness of

125

ruined Aachen, where the only promise Hitler now held out to his followers was one of certain death. The Nazi dream was fading. What had seemed to them glorious was now hideous. Ugliness, foulness, and despair had taken over.

II. SURRENDER

AACHEN, GERMANY
Saturday, October 21, 1944

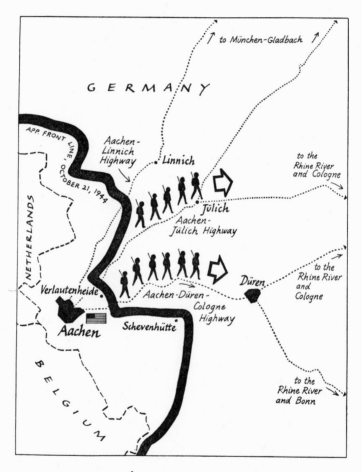

ON TO THE RHINE!

CHAPTER 11

A T 2400 (midnight), Wednesday, October 18, a three-man outpost from King (K) Company, 18th Infantry, guarding the path up a ridge near Crucifix Hill in the vicinity of Verlautenheide, was aroused by noises coming from the darkness at the foot of the slope.

Atop the crest, King Company stood fully alert; three vicious German counterattacks had been beaten off only hours before. The Yanks had inflicted terrible casualties on the enemy, and since dusk no German activity had been reported except for indications that the foe was pulling out of his positions and retreating to the east.

However, despite this good news, King Company was

taking no chances. The company was ready for any thrust by the foe. The sounds heard by the outpost at midnight were reported to the Company CP, and King Company's CO rushed a squad of riflemen to reinforce the OP. Machine gunners and mortar crews stood by prepared to open fire instantly.

Out of the night someone called, "Hey, anybody up on the hill?" The voice was American.

"Who wants to know?" the outpost's sergeant asked.

"Patrol from King Company, One-hundred and nineteenth Infantry, Thirtieth Division," the same voice said.

"Give the password," snapped the sergeant.

"Rosebud."

"Keep the home fires burning," the sergeant said, tensely awaiting the countersign.

"Till the boys come home," the proper retort swiftly followed from the bottom.

"Come on in with your hands high," the sergeant said.

Six GIs scrambled into the 18th Infantry position. Someone flicked on a hooded flashlight. He turned the beam on the grinning 119th Infantry doughboys.

"What outfit is this?" a man of the patrol asked.

"King Company, Eighteenth," the sergeant responded.

"Takes King Company every time," the patrol member laughed.

"How come you were so long getting here? What've you been doing, playing gin rummy?" an 18th Infantry GI asked.

"Buddy, we wanted to get here weeks ago but the

Krauts had other ideas. Anyway, we're here. Better late than never, I always say."

The following morning at dawn, powerful 2nd Armored Division task forces and Red Battalion, 119th Infantry, welded the fragile link between the 1st and 30th Divisions into an unbroken chain around Aachen. The Germans attacked wildly from the east to break the encirclement, but every assault was repulsed; and by Friday, October 20, the Germans stopped trying to break through.

By then, even Field Marshal Walther Model realized that despite Hitler's orders Aachen could no longer be held. The Field Marshal should have radioed Colonel Wilck giving him permission to surrender. However, Model was more Nazi than soldier. Instead of allowing Wilck to capitulate and stop the sacrifice of German lives, the Marshal sent a message of another sort to the Aachen commander:

"Powerful forces are on the way to raise the siege of Aachen and destroy the American gangsters. Hold on, Wilck! I have this day promoted you to the rank of Brigadier General. . . ."

Although Colonel Wilck was pleased by his promotion, it did little to ease his predicament. Earlier, he had retreated with his staff and about four hundred soldiers into a massive stone building on Jakobstrasse, a block from the ruins of the Quellenhof Hotel.

In happier times, the headquarters had been a furniture warehouse. Its walls were eight feet thick and the basement went thirty feet underground. Even a direct hit from a Long Tom or a bomb could not penetrate the structure, which had withstood all the shelling and bombing without damage.

Wilck had converted the former warehouse into a command post bunker. He had it ventilated and lighted by electricity. Kitchens, sleeping quarters, and sanitary facilities for a thousand persons had been installed. But since the big American bombardment ten days earlier, there had been neither water nor power.

The bunker had to be lighted by candles and kerosene lamps; telephone lines were out, and only a battery-operated transmitter-receiver brought news from the outside. With the electricity gone, the ventilation system failed and the air inside the building grew fetid; the drinking water was limited to rain caught in buckets and tarpaulins spread on the roof. Sanitary conditions became intolerable as raw sewage from broken pipes seeped into the basement. This contaminated flood inundated food storage bins. Everyone in the bunker was unwashed, hungry, dirty, and wretched.

Outside, in the ravaged streets, troops of Blue Battalion, 26th Infantry, were mopping up a few scraps of German resistance. Most of Wilck's original five-thousand-man garrison had been killed, wounded, or captured. In the shrinking enclave still held by the Germans, discipline was nonexistent. Drunken SS men reeled about, shooting at civilians and Wehrmacht soldiers who fired back. Bloody brawls raged between Wehrmacht and SS.

Terrified Volkssturmers ripped off their arm bands,

threw away their weapons, and fled to the Americans. Gangs of looters scrabbled in the ruins of private homes, and men were killed battling over worthless baubles.

As one 26th Infantry officer observed, "Aachen was like a huge insane asylum. The Germans lost pride, dignity, and self-respect. They crept to us like whipped dogs. . . ."

Finally, on Saturday, October 21, at 1000 (10:00 A.M.) Colonel Wilck gathered his staff in a room on an upper floor of the warehouse. Less than two hundred yards away Blue Battalion GIs were taking the last German strongpoints.

Wilck announced to his officers that further resistance was impossible. He then transmitted by radio a message of devotion to Hitler. After this was done, Wilck prepared to surrender.

Among the inmates of the warehouse headquarters were thirty-two American prisoners. Two U. S. sergeants were sent out into the street carrying a white flag. Behind them came the rest of the American captives and Colonel Wilck with his staff. The nearest American unit was a platoon from King (K) Company, 26th Infantry, commanded by twenty-one-year-old Second Lieutenant Winfred Short, to whom Wilck surrendered.

Short summoned his battalion commander, Lieutenant Colonel John T. Corley, who negotiated the capitulation. Through an interpreter, Wilck asked for terms.

"No terms but unconditional surrender," Corley said brusquely.

Wilck sighed. His shoulders sagged. "I have no choice."

133

"No, sir, you do not," Corley declared.

"Then I accept," Wilck murmured.

At 1100 (11:00 A.M.), the German soldiers filed out of the headquarters building and were disarmed by Corley's men. A few minutes later, all fighting ended in Aachen. The Germans stood in a dejected huddle.

Colonel Wilck was escorted to Corley's jeep. "May I address my men?" the conquered German requested.

"Go ahead." Corley nodded. "But no Nazi speeches!"

Standing up in the rear of the jeep, Wilck faced his beaten soldiers. In a voice often cracked with emotion, the gray-haired German commander said:

"My soldiers! I am speaking to you at a painful moment. I was forced to surrender because we ran out of ammunition, food, and water. . . . I saw future fighting was useless. . . . I acted against orders, for I was supposed to fight to the last man and the last cartridge. . . . However, I could not bear to see another one of my brave men fall and I surrendered. . . . The Americans refuse to let us give a Sieg Heil and to say Heil Hitler . . . but we can still do it in our minds. . . ."

Wilck saluted the men and sat down. The jeep shot away, jouncing over the rubble. After a few moments, Colonel Wilck turned to Corley. In heavily-accented English the defeated Aachen commander slowly said, "Germany is lost. Hitler is a madman. Nothing can save us. If only we had never followed him. . . ."

"You should have thought of that much sooner, Colonel," Corley said.

At noon, Saturday, October 21, the American flag was

raised over the shell of Aachen's fire-gutted city hall. The battle was over, the city taken. The Germans had suffered a serious psychological handicap in addition to losing an important city. Hitler had vowed that no enemy soldiers would ever stand on German soil—but the Americans were there. He had sworn Aachen would not be taken. The Americans had captured the city. The Fuehrer had reassured the Germans that the Westwall, the impregnable Siegfried line, could not be broken. The Americans had smashed through it.

Now as never before the Germans saw that their Fuehrer was fallible. Aachen had fallen and the Siegfried line had been breached. All the German courage, devotion, and sacrifice had not been enough. Aachen was in American hands. And the smoke rising from the fires of the ravaged city spread a cloud over Germany, a harbinger of what was to befall the nation whose leaders and people had dreamed of ruling the world.

The road into the heart of Germany lay open to the Americans, but before they traversed that road, many of the boys who watched the Stars and Stripes raised over Aachen would be dead or wounded.

Terrible battles still faced them: Huertgen Forest, the Ardennes, the Rhine River crossing. Now, as they stood in ruined Aachen, the young Americans gave no heed to future trials. They had youth and strength and the confidence that one day, sooner or later, they would destroy Nazi Germany and the men who had created that monstrous nation.

The Americans strolled about Aachen looking over

the destruction they had wrought. None regretted what they saw. "We'll keep on clobbering Germany until Hitler is finished and the Germans really understand the price of war," a GI told the *New York Times* correspondent.

"Yeah. Just tell the folks back home we'll keep fighting until hell freezes over if we have to," another soldier said.

A third Yank smiled. "Sure. All I need is a shower." He added wistfully, "I haven't had one since way back in September."

On Sunday, October 22, the U. S. troops plodded out of Aachen in the rain. On that cold, dismal morning the war seemed far from over and peace only a beautiful hope that lived in the hearts of men. But the men marched onward, heading eastward toward Cologne and the Rhine, moving step by step to the end of the war.

BRIEF GLOSSARY
OF MILITARY TERMS

AA	Antiaircraft
AMG	Allied Military Government
AT	Antitank
Bn	Battalion
CO	Commanding Officer
CP	Command Post
HE	High explosive
Luftwaffe	German Air Force
OP	Outpost
Panzer	Armored vehicles, especially tanks
SA	Sturmabteilung (Storm Troopers)
SOS	Services of Supply
SPG	Self-propelled gun—a heavy-caliber cannon mounted on tank treads
SS	Schutzstaffel (German Elite Corps)
SS Waffentruppen	SS Combat Troops
Wehrmacht	German Regular Army

GERMAN AND AMERICAN FORCES
THAT PARTICIPATED
IN THE BATTLE OF AACHEN

GERMAN:

SEVENTH ARMY

LXXIV Corps with attached troops
LXXXI Corps with attached troops
LVII Panzer Corps with attached troops

2nd SS Waffen Division
1st SS Panzer Division
9th SS Panzer Division
12th SS Panzer Division
116th Panzer Division

246th Infantry Regiment
352nd Infantry Regiment
404th Infantry Regiment
689th Infantry Regiment
1st SS Panzer Grenadier Regiment

AMERICAN:

    U. S. FIRST ARMY (*Lieutenant General Courtney H. Hodges*)

    V CORPS (*Major General Leonard Grerow*)

4th Infantry Division
28th Infantry Division
5th Armored Division

    VII CORPS (*Major General J. Lawton Collins*)

1st Infantry Division
9th Infantry Division
3rd Armored Division

    XIX CORPS (*Major General Charles Corlett*)

29th Infantry Division
30th Infantry Division
2nd Armored Division
7th Armored Division

BIBLIOGRAPHY

In gathering material for this book, I consulted letters and diaries of private individuals, unit histories, and journals not generally available to the reader. Of the sources easily accessible, I found the following most useful:

BOOKS, OFFICIAL REPORTS, AND UNIT HISTORIES

Baumgartner, John W., Lt., and others, *The 16th Infantry Regiment: 1798–1946*. 1946.

Call Me Spearhead: Saga of the Third Armored Division. Paris (Stars and Stripes), 1944.

Ewing, Joseph H., *29, Let's Go! A History of the 29th Infantry Division in World War II*. Washington, D.C., Infantry Journal Press, 1948.

First U. S. Army Report of Operations Data: 1 August 1944 —22 February 1945. Washington, D.C., 1945.

Heidenheimer, Arnold, *Vanguard to Victory: History of the 18th Infantry*. 1954.

Hewitt, Robert L., *Work Horse of the Western Front: The Story of the 30th Infantry Division*. Washington, D.C., Infantry Journal Press, 1946.

History of the Third Armored Division: April 1941—July 1958, A. Darmstadt (Stars and Stripes), 1959.

Knickerbocker, H. R., and others, *Danger Forward: The Story of the First Division in World War II*. Washington, D.C., Society of the 1st Division, 1948.

Mission Accomplished: The Story of the VII Corps, U. S. Army, 1944–1945.

NEWSPAPERS
(September–October, 1944)

New York Herald Tribune
New York Post
The New York Times
New York World-Telegram
Stars and Stripes

PERIODICALS
(September–October–November, 1944)

Collier's
Life
Newsweek
Time
Yank, the Army Weekly

INDEX

ABOUT THE AUTHOR

Irving Werstein has made writing both his goal and his life. His dedication to his career has been constant. Even when he was officially a factory worker, a salesman, or an actor, Mr. Werstein spent his free moments writing. After serving in the U. S. Army from 1941–1945 he resumed his writing. By 1938, he had given up side jobs and devoted all his time to writing. He has written magazine stories, television and radio scripts, and several books. Although he has taken related courses at Columbia University, the New School, and New York University, Mr. Werstein believes that "the best school for writing is life itself."

He was born in Brooklyn, New York, and spent his school years in Richmond Hill, Long Island. He has also lived in Mexico, Italy, and England, and has traveled to Holland and Denmark. Mr. Werstein, his wife, and his son live in Stuyvesant Town in lower Manhattan. The Wersteins are addicted to city life and find it "especially delightful in rainy or snowy weather!"